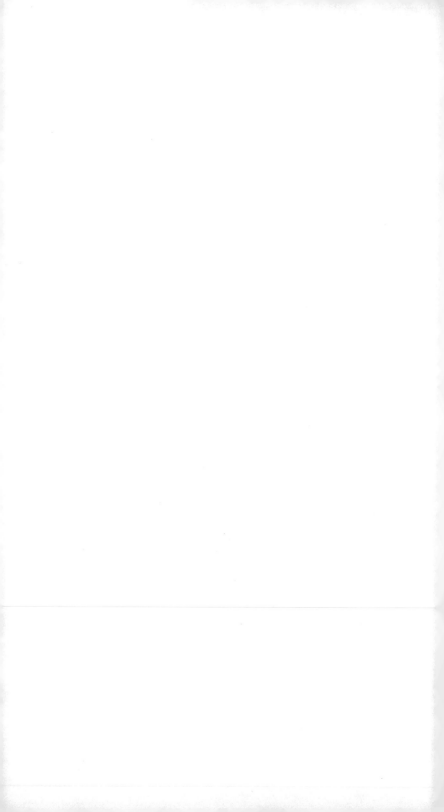

The National Collegiate Athletic Association

The National Collegiate Athletic Association

A Study in Cartel Behavior

Arthur A. Fleisher III
Brian L. Goff
and
Robert D. Tollison

The University of Chicago Press · Chicago and London

Arthur A. Fleisher III is assistant professor of economics at Metropolitan State College, Denver, Colorado.
Brian L. Goff is associate professor of economics at Western Kentucky University, Bowling Green.
Robert D. Tollison is the Duncan Black professor of economics and the director of the Center for the Study of Public Choice at George Mason University, Fairfax, Virginia.

The University of Chicago Press, Chicago 60637
The University of Chicago Press, Ltd., London
© 1992 by The University of Chicago
All rights reserved. Published 1992
Printed in the United States of America
00 99 98 97 96 95 94 93 92   5 4 3 2 1

ISBN 0–226–25326–0 (cloth)

Library of Congress Cataloging-in-Publication Data

Fleisher, Arthur A.
    The National Collegiate Athletic Association : a study in cartel behavior / Arthur A. Fleisher, Brian L. Goff, and Robert D. Tollison.
        p.   cm.
    Includes bibliographical references and index.
    1. National Collegiate Athletic Association—Finance.
2. Cartels—United States—Case studies.   3. College sports—Economic aspects—United States—Case studies.   I. Goff, Brian L.   II. Tollison, Robert D.   III. Title.
GV350.F58   1992
338.4'3796'071173 — dc20   91-26437
                                                  CIP

♾ The paper used in this publication meets the minimum requirements of the American National Standard for Information Sciences—Permanence of Paper for Printed Library Materials, ANSI Z39.48–1984.

CONTENTS

List of Illustrations   vii

List of Tables   ix

Preface   xi

Introduction   1

1   The NCAA as a Cartel   4

2   Economic Theory and the NCAA   17

3   A Synoptic History of the NCAA   35

4   Inside the NCAA   66

5   NCAA Enforcement   100

6   NCAA Academic Requirements as Barriers to Entry   123

7   Capture of the NCAA Regulatory Process   133

8   The State of NCAA Policy   144

Appendixes   163

Bibliography   177

Index   183

ILLUSTRATIONS

1 Organization of the NCAA 70

2 Winning Percentage of NCAA Violators 113

3 NCAA Repeat Offenders: University of Houston 116

4 NCAA Repeat Offenders: University of Kansas 117

5 NCAA Repeat Offenders: Southern Methodist University 117

TABLES

1	Stadium Construction for Selected Institutions	43
2	NCAA Television Contracts, 1952–83	53
3	Total College Football Attendance, 1948–89	54
4	NCAA Membership, 1906–88	67
5	Aggregate Revenues as Reported by the NCAA for Class A Schools	75
6	Frequency Distribution of Athletic Revenues for Major Schools in 1985	75
7	1989 Football Attendance and Estimated Gate Receipts	76
8	1983 Network Television Football Revenues by Conference	77
9	Estimated Network Television Revenues by School, 1984	78
10	Estimated Alumni Contributions to Athletics, 1986	79
11	1989 National Collegiate Division I Men's Basketball Championship: Analysis of Distribution of Net Receipts	81
12	Growth in Bowl Receipts per Team from 1968–69 through 1988–89	82
13	Athletic Expenses, 1973–84, and Percentage Breakdown for 1985 for Class A Schools	83
14	Annual Compensation of Football and Basketball Coaches and Athletic Directors as of 1986	85
15	University of Michigan Reported Athletic Finances, 1989	86
16	NCAA Football Enforcement Actions, 1953–83	106

17 LOGIT Analysis of NCAA Enforcement
Actions 110
18 Changes in Mean Winning Percentage Based
on NCAA Enforcement Actions 115
19 Enforcement Actions against Six Traditional
Athletic Powers 120
20 Descriptive Statistics 129
21 LOGIT Analysis of Votes for SAT/GPA
Sliding Scale 130
22 LOGIT Analysis of Votes for Proposition 42 131
23 LOGIT Estimate of Membership 141
24 NCAA Council Membership of Eight Major
Programs, 1952–77 142

PREFACE

Most consumers of college athletics do not concern themselves with the National Collegiate Athletic Association, except when it comes calling on their favorite school and puts the school on probation for recruiting violations, thereby denying the school television and bowl appearances and scholarships for its athletes. At this point the NCAA becomes something akin to Darth Vader, a dark influence on college athletics possessing seemingly endless power with no provisions for due process. Discussions at tailgating parties turn to such issues as, since virtually everyone violates the recruiting rules, why was our school singled out for detection and probation? Inevitably, the answer to such questions centers on competitor schools, usually located within the same recruiting locale. Hypothetically, North Carolina, which has a large influence in the NCAA, turns in South Carolina, which does not, and has it placed on probation. North Carolina then defeats South Carolina on the playing field for the next dozen years because South Carolina is limited in its recruiting of athletes. This book gives structure and empirical support to this hypothesis about NCAA enforcement practices.

Several individuals deserve thanks for their contributions to our study. William F. Shughart II worked with us at the initial stages of research and provided us valuable advice at many turns. Robert E. McCormick supplied us with useful comments and with several useful papers related to our study. Melvin Boreland and Robert Pulsinelli's work on college athletic finances was helpful to us. Additionally, discussions with and comments from the following individuals aided our study: Richard Cantrell, Kevin Grier, Roy Howsen, Tom Wisely, and two anonymous reviewers. We also thank Carol Robert for her assistance in the preparation of the manuscript.

INTRODUCTION

T he purpose of this book is to study the National Collegiate Athletic Association (NCAA) as a cartel. Such a research program may seem strange or puzzling. Nonetheless,
as we hope the reader will discover, the cartel perspective provides a unifying means of explaining the behavior of colleges
and universities with respect to their athletic programs over
the last several decades. Moreover, that perspective helps to
answer such questions as: How did the NCAA become a cartel?
What factors contributed to its success? Why do illicit payments to athletes seem so persistent? What is the economic
value of a college athlete? Why are some schools placed on
probation and others not? and Why are academic eligibility
requirements (like the much discussed Proposition 48) passed
by the NCAA? In other words, even though some observers
may be uncomfortable with the idea that the NCAA is a cartel,
the actual proof will be in the pudding—does cartel theory
offer a useful explanation of NCAA behavior?

Chapter 1 sets the stage for the study, discussing why it is
reasonable to claim that the NCAA is a cartel and why the
NCAA affords an unusual opportunity for economists to study
a process of cartelization.

Chapter 2 lays the theoretical groundwork for analyzing the
NCAA in cartel terms. Technical rigor is purposely kept to a
minimum, but the essentials of cartel theory as they apply to
the NCAA are spelled out.

Chapter 3 provides a brief history of the NCAA from its
founding around the turn of the century to the most recent
developments surrounding the organization. Important decisions and events are highlighted. The narrative history is organized around the economic theory of organizations and car-

tels, and the evolution of the NCAA from a problem-solving association into a rent-producing cartel is recorded. As with many similar organizations, the original startup costs were borne for one reason (problem solving), but once the NCAA was organized, the marginal costs of acting as a group in other directions (such as cartelization) were very low. Special attention is given to the late 1940s and early 1950s, when this transformation into a cartel became complete.

Chapter 4 surveys the internal organization of the NCAA. This chapter is a behavioral perspective on the NCAA. The association's organizational structure is explored as well as the specific rules which serve as the means for its control of the cartel. The workings of NCAA enforcement processes and specific applications of cartel rules are covered in some detail. In addition, this chapter provides an array of descriptive statistics about NCAA revenues, rules, sanctions, and trends in selected variables of organizational interest. In particular, estimates of per-school revenue from athletics and of the value of college athletes to universities are provided.

Chapter 5 draws on the cartel theory presented in chapter 2 to advance a theory of NCAA enforcement actions. The theory stresses the indirect and probabilistic ways in which cheating on the cartel rules is detected and advances a redistributive hypothesis with respect to who wins and who loses from NCAA enforcement. For example, to determine whether a team is cheating, competition schools will observe its on-field performance rather than search for canceled checks from illegal payments to athletes. Thus, other things equal, the variability of a school's winning percentage is a signal of the amount of cheating by the school. When a team that has not won the conference championship for years suddenly becomes better and wins, it becomes a suspect for recruiting violations and a candidate for eventual NCAA probation. In this way the NCAA functions to protect the rents of perennial athletic powers. This theory is tested on data for college football and found to be a useful explanation of which major football programs have been placed on probation in the modern era of the NCAA.

Chapter 6 uses the economic theory of voting to study NCAA behavior. In particular, a voting hypothesis concerning the much discussed Propositions 48 and 42 is developed and tested. This NCAA legislation, which imposed more rigid academic requirements on student athletes, was voted on by NCAA members. This chapter analyzes these proposals as cartel devices intended to transfer wealth among conferences and member schools. Specifically, the data suggest that NCAA voting tends to move the benefits from schools with lesser academic reputations to institutions with well-established academic reputations, especially at the level of the athletic conferences.

In chapter 7, a hypothesis about the membership of key NCAA committees is developed from the basic cartel theory. The hypothesis suggests that key NCAA enforcement committees have been controlled over time by schools which had strong athletic programs in the early 1950s, when the modern NCAA cartel apparatus was established. Old football powers, for example, were therefore "grandfathered" into control of the NCAA, providing a mechanism whereby the rents of such programs could be protected and sustained by placing potential entrants on probation. The evidence presented in this chapter shows that membership can be explained by historical winning percentage, as suggested by cartel theory.

Chapter 8 discusses the role of various participants, including players, fans, and the media, in discussions of possible reform of the NCAA. The general issue addressed is why there is so little interest, in general, in market-oriented reform of the NCAA, and, in particular, reform in the spirit of economic analysis, which would suggest paying players the value of their marginal products.

The methodology of the book is based on positive economics. Theories are presented and tested. The goal is to understand how this fascinating organization, the NCAA, actually works. Perhaps the arguments presented will have relevance for potential reform in that reform can proceed from a more fully informed perspective about how the NCAA functions and what its reality actually is.

O N E

The NCAA as a Cartel

College sports command a great deal of enthusiasm and attention from fans. Increasingly, however, not all of the excitement and interest comes from competition on the playing field. Payments and other inducements to college athletes, agent-player relationships, alumni intervention, performance-enhancing drugs, and questions of racial bias have most recently been in the media spotlight on intercollegiate athletics. Moreover, during the last forty years, college sports have grown from a small cottage industry into a business grossing over $1 billion in revenues per year. The question of whether or not college sports are a business is no longer relevant; the question is only one of the order of magnitude. Secrecy and the presence of in-kind benefits prevent exact estimation of institutional athletic revenues, but even conservatively, revenues from athletics for some schools approach $15 to $20 million per year. Television rights for various events run into the hundreds of millions of dollars per year. Football gate receipts at the University of Michigan, where seating capacity is 106,000, approach $10 million per year. Alumni contributions per school often reach several millions of dollars each year. Schools have also increased utilization of their brand names on paraphernalia ranging from sweaters and hats to mugs. Coaches have shared in these increased revenues. Base coaching salaries have grown into six figures at many major schools, and often head coaches earn more from outside endorsements, television programs, and shoe contracts than from their base salaries. Illicit payments notwithstanding, however, the NCAA has effectively kept athlete remuneration at the in-kind level of a scholarship, room and board, and incidentals. Schools and coaches have prospered; athletes have not.

Everyone is aware that college sports generate large sums of money and economic opportunities; yet a distinction is usually drawn between college and professional sports. Because of the explicit, for-profit status of professional sports, the public and the media recognize and generally accept profit-driven behavior in the case of participants in professional sports. The non-profit, educational setting of college sports helps to mask much of its underlying profit-motivated behavior. Commonly, the NCAA is viewed as a benign administrator of the rules of college athletics. This perspective recognizes many of the problems and perverse outcomes which result from NCAA rules and actions; yet these outcomes are usually attributed to short-sightedness, ignorance, or the greed of certain elements within the organization.

In contrast, economists generally view the NCAA as a cartel.[1] They hold this view because the NCAA has historically devised rules to restrict output (the number of games played and televised) and to restrict competition for inputs (student-athletes). Economists have focused primarily on the input or monopsonistic aspects of NCAA behavior. NCAA rules concerning recruiting and financial aid are seen as transferring rewards from players to schools and coaches, and the rules are seen as an expression of an agreement among buyers to restrict competition for inputs. These points are well established in the literature, and, indeed, it could be observed that the NCAA has obtained much more durable returns on its cartel behavior than other, more notable cartels such as OPEC.

The purpose of this book is to extend the analysis of the NCAA as a cartel and to probe its inner workings and organization. How is this cartel enforced? Who are the key regulators? Which schools are put on probation and why? How do member schools vote on rule changes? What is the nature of rent distribution within the NCAA? How does this complex cartel function? Answering such questions represents the central tasks of this book.

---

1. For a brief exposition of this position, see Becker (1985, 1987) and Mc-Cormick and Meiners (1987).

1. Why Study the NCAA?

Economics has a well-developed theory of cartel behavior. Textbook models show the optimal price and quantity solution and the subsequent distribution of cartel rewards (rents) among colluding industry members. Also, the theory identifies the constraints that impinge on the collective process of maximizing cartel profits. Heterogeneous costs and products among producers hinder successful collusion. The same profits that encourage cartelization attract potential entrants, as well as entice cartel members to violate the agreement. Antitrust laws and their enforcement increase transaction costs to cartel members by increasing the importance of secrecy and increasing the possible punitive legal costs.

In spite of an accepted theoretical foundation, few in-depth empirical studies of cartels exist. The reasons for this are apparent. The illegality of most collusive agreements discourages the existence of cartels. When collusive agreements are made, their illegality drives them underground, and even without the problem of illegality and secrecy, firm-level data are often difficult to obtain for participants in a cartel. Because of these problems, the most public examples of cartel behavior are found beyond the grasp of U.S. antitrust policy. The DeBeers cartel of diamond producers and the cartel of oil-producing nations (OPEC) are two of the more prominent contemporary cases.

The NCAA provides a useful setting for applications and tests of cartel theory. The NCAA operates largely, though not entirely, without antitrust constraints so that it has a long and to a large extent public history. In the *National Collegiate Athletic Association v. Board of Regents of the University of Oklahoma et al.* (1984), the association ran afoul of U.S. antitrust laws (more on this case later). In spite of this ruling, the NCAA continues to restrict output (other than through television rights) and to regulate competition for inputs. The NCAA does not have a legislative exemption from antitrust laws; still, it has had two factors that have worked in its favor with respect to its legal status and its ability to continue to behave as a cartel. First, sports in the United States have historically been given a great deal of leeway in terms of their treatment under the antitrust laws.[2] Federal courts largely ignored or sidestepped antitrust issues in sports until the 1970s and the onset of unionization by professional athletes. Second, the NCAA is strongly linked to higher education and traditions of amateurism. Member schools have successfully hidden cartel behavior behind the rhetoric of support for academic achievement and the nonproprietary setting of universities.

A further advantage in the empirical study of the NCAA is the amount of school- (firm-) specific data that are publicly available. A vast number of statistical data have been collected on sports events and related activities. Also, the fact that the firms are educational institutions (in most cases, publicly operated) leads to more published data than are normally available on proprietary firms.

2. Key Issues in a Cartel Study of the NCAA
Is the NCAA Really a Cartel?

The question of whether an association of rival producers implies cartel-like behavior is debatable. Some industrial cooperation may function to establish standard weights, measures, or the like, which provide benefits to producers and consumers. Even among economists, the cartel interpretation of the NCAA has met some strenuous objection.[3] McKenzie and Sullivan (1985) suggest that the association is a necessary vehicle for scheduling, rules standardization, and provision of amateur standards. In this view, while a few star players may have value to their schools in excess of their in-kind compensation, the same condition does not hold for the average college player. What can be said about this argument?[4]

First, a convincing prima facie case that the NCAA is a cartel can be derived from the explicit behavior of the NCAA. The open collusion among schools extends far beyond rules stan-

---

2. Noll (1974) provides a collection of articles on the relationship between government and the sports industry up to the early 1970s. Cairns, Jennet, and Sloane (1986) further update the antitrust environment of professional sports.

3. See McKenzie and Sullivan (1985).

4. See Browning and Browning (1989, pp. 504–10) for a brief overview of the evidence of cartel behavior by the NCAA.

dardization. For example, the contract with a single television network, until recently voided by the Supreme Court, was not necessary for rules standardization. It restricted competition among members and increased NCAA revenues. The NCAA Football Television Committee Report clearly recognized the lost revenues and increased coverage of college football resulting from the Supreme Court decision.[5]

Second, while revenues to schools, coaches' salaries, and expenditures on athletic programs have exploded over the years since 1950, allowable compensation to athletes has remained essentially the same: a full grant-in-aid equal to tuition and fees, room and board, and books. Any athlete receiving more than a full grant-in-aid is automatically ineligible for NCAA participation. This differential growth in allowable compensation is easy to explain with cartel theory. Schools have successfully colluded to restrict growth in student-athlete compensation to levels below the value of these athletes to the schools. A noncartel explanation of such developments is not so obvious. Such a framework must explain the huge increases in the compensation of two inputs (schools and coaches), while players' compensation has remained almost constant (in real terms) over the same period of time. In a cartel, rent-redistribution framework, this seeming paradox vanishes.

Third, the exclusion of school brand-name and other capital assets from NCAA regulation also suggests a cartel scheme. Proponents of the NCAA restrictions have pointed to educational requirements, standardized rules, and maintenance of amateurism as rationales for such things as the television plan and eligibility rules. Yet that NCAA policy is not consistent across all types of inputs automatically accords certain advantages to some schools in recruiting and performance. Specifically, one can point to stadiums, training facilities, food, living accommodations, and the like as examples of unregulated physical capital across schools. If a quest for education, amateurism, and standardized rules were truly at the heart of NCAA behavior, these inputs would be regulated along with

5. See National Collegiate Athletic Association, *1984 NCAA Football Television Committee Report* (1985, pp. 18–19).

labor inputs. Indeed, if such purposes were a goal of the NCAA, then some schools would not be allowed to offer recruits a more attractive package of complements than other schools, and student athletes would not be allowed to choose schools freely. Indeed, athletes might be subject to a draft system, as are some professional athletes.

Fourth, the value of many athletes to schools or their marginal revenue products (MRPs) are large in relation to the market value of the educational product that they are given, at least in football and basketball. College athletes possess skills which are relatively rare in the population as a whole and are in demand by a large segment of sports fans. Conservative estimates of the career MRPs of certain college athletes, such as Patrick Ewing, Doug Flutie, or Bo Jackson, are in the millions of dollars and over $10 million in some cases. Certainly, the MRP of the average "starter" in college football or basketball is less than this; yet average salaries in the same professional sports, which run into the hundreds of thousands of dollars per year, provide a rough shadow price for, at least, the largest revenue producers in college sports. Even if the average college player's MRP is one-quarter of that of the average professional player, the in-kind educational compensation of college players falls several times short of this level. This issue is explored further in chapter 4.

Fifth, the very existence of illicit payments indicates the presence of rents attempting to find their way to the relevant input. Producers and loyal patrons of Burger King do not offer large cash and in-kind enticements to lure skillful workers away from McDonald's. If college athletics are in financial deficit, as is often claimed, such illicit enticements to athletes would not make any sense.

The available evidence of price-fixing, output controls, compensation of athletes below their MRPs, the absence of regulation of brand-name and capital assets, and so on, taken together indicate cartel behavior. If these behavioral aspects do not suggest a cartel, one could fairly ask, what would? In this case it seems that there is no evidence short of fanciful tape recordings of Dick Schultz (the present executive director of the NCAA) and the NCAA Council reviewing graphs of monopsony theory that would refute the no-cartel proposition.

The Source of NCAA Power

In spite of the evidence that the NCAA behaves as a cartel, some questions linger as to the source of the NCAA's cartel power. Clearly, athletes are not forced to accept scholarship offers nor are schools forced to join the NCAA. One key factor contributing to the NCAA's monopoly power is U.S. antitrust policy. As noted earlier, the sports industry in the United States has historically enjoyed lenient antitrust treatment. This is especially so with respect to college sports. The impact of antitrust enforcement upon NCAA collusive power is clearly seen in the recent decision on the NCAA television plan (*National Collegiate Athletic Association v. Board of Regents of the University of Oklahoma et al.*, 1984). Before the Supreme Court decision, with relative immunity from antitrust laws, the NCAA enforced a television plan that severely limited the total number of games that could be broadcast per season, limited the number of appearances per school, and increased NCAA revenues from television rights. In the wake of the decision, the output of college football to consumers in terms of the number of games televised per weekend increased dramatically, as did the quality of the matchups presented. Before the decision, a fan might be able to see two or sometimes three games per weekend. Since the decision, Saturdays have provided morning to night college football coverage. Of course, this is exactly what economic theory predicts when a market shifts from monopoly to competition. Quantity (number of televised games) increases and price (payment by the networks per game) falls. It is not a great leap to suggest that the lenient posture of antitrust policy toward the NCAA input restrictions for student athletes serves a similar function in maintaining the NCAA's monopsony power.

Lenient antitrust policy provides a necessary condition for successful collusion; yet, given that the NCAA is a voluntary association, its antitrust status alone is not a sufficient condition for long-lasting monopoly or monopsony power. Two other factors provide this condition. One factor is the discontinuous, or "lumpy," entry condition in college athletics. One or even a few schools cannot produce a viable ten- or eleven-game football season or a thirty-game basketball season. Coordination among several schools would be necessary for a successful breakaway from the NCAA and establishment of a competitive league or association. In other words, there is a first-mover problem. While this does not render disassociation from the NCAA and new competitive entry impossible, it does increase the costs and decrease the likelihood of such behavior.

A second factor plays a major role in keeping schools in the NCAA.[6] This is the threat of sanctions against a school's *academic* programs. Obviously, the NCAA does not directly control the academic accreditation process; however, NCAA sanctions and pressure have influenced this process. For instance, in the early 1950s Oklahoma A&M (now Oklahoma State) fell under NCAA scrutiny because of its athletic scholarships. Because of these scholarships, the North Central College and Secondary Schools Association, compiled a report on the school and considered repealing its accreditation. Alchian and Allen (1969) mention a similar episode.[7] A school placed on probation will be less likely to exit the cartel if, by exiting, they draw upon themselves the threat of academic sanctions. Moreover, many conferences are not just simply athletic affiliations but are also academic associations operated directly by university presidents. Also, organizationally, the NCAA does not separate athletics and academics. The NCAA Council and Infractions Committee are not staffed simply by coaches and athletic directors. Faculty, deans, and college executives fill these positions. Thus, the NCAA can threaten the brand-name capital of academic institutions in such a fundamental way as to make exit from the association very costly. Loss of accreditation would seriously harm many schools in the market for

---

6. See *New York Times*, April 5, 1953 (Section V, p. 3).

7. Alchian and Allen (1969, pp. 522–523) asked the question, "What rewards of membership in the collusion are greater than the advantages obtainable by not belonging, so that the threat of membership cancellation can be effective in enforcing the agreement?" They mentioned that even Phi Beta Kappa refused to authorize chapters at some schools that used excessive amounts of resources for athletic scholarships. They also pointed out that a school's accreditation could be jeopardized for NCAA infractions. These costs to the school reverberate into higher costs of recruiting and retaining faculty members and students.

students, endowments, and grants. The linkage between academics and athletics would seem to be the real source of the NCAA's cartel power.

Interschool Struggles in College Athletics

The implicit transfer of funds away from athletes is not the entire NCAA cartel story. The distribution of rewards within a cartel is not necessarily done on an egalitarian basis, and the NCAA is no exception in this regard. Schools compete with each other in a number of ways, inside and outside regulated areas, to capture these benefits. Some succeed in altering some of the mechanisms which determine their share of cartel rewards.

One such outcome is present in NCAA enforcement practices. Even cursory observations indicate that the enforcement process is not evenhanded. The same types of behavior do not always receive the same penalties. Texas Christian University was placed on a three-year probation with severe scholarship reductions and had to refund revenues because of football violations it discovered and reported. Moreover, the coach dismissed the guilty players in mid-season. In contrast, over twenty ex-University of Kentucky basketball players were reported to have acknowledged receiving illegal payments. The NCAA could not find sufficient evidence to bring sanctions in this case. Later, only after $1,000 was discovered in a package sent to a recruit, did the NCAA impose sanctions on the University of Kentucky basketball program.

The interschool competition for rewards is also seen in the support of and opposition to rules which mandate eligibility across institutions. Supposedly, such rules are supported for reasons of academic integrity, fairness, support for the idea of true student athletes, and the like. However, a more likely and common motivation is the attempt to gain a competitive advantage. For instance, in the 1960s a rule was proposed which would have required all athletes to maintain a 1.6 grade point average. Interestingly, the institutions with the highest academic reputations, the Ivy League schools, dissented in this case. They supported eligibility rules, but on a per-school rather than an NCAA basis. Not surprisingly, recent attempts at instituting eligibility requirements are usually supported most strongly by the schools which have large resources devoted to tutoring student athletes, such as the University of Michigan, which spent more than $250,000 on tutoring in 1986.

Stability of the NCAA

In recent years, college athletics has experienced dramatic increases in popularity, attendance, and revenues. In spite of this, the NCAA faces a seemingly turbulent future. Member schools have strained the NCAA's one-time stability. The challenge to the single television package by Oklahoma and Georgia is a prime example of this type of behavior. More recently, Notre Dame's break with the College Football Association's network television package further demonstrates the tenuous bonds holding the NCAA together.[8] In addition, athletes have become more restless. More are choosing to leave college early; more are accepting illicit payments. Congress and state legislatures have shown an interest in dealing with issues related to college athletics. All of these currents in college athletics grow out of forces and competition within a cartel, as discussed in chapter 2.

Unique Characteristics of the NCAA

The subsequent chapters address many issues concerning the cartel behavior of the NCAA. Along the way, analogies are drawn between NCAA activity and production in other industries, especially professional sports. Some will object to these analogies and to phrases such as "wage rates," "profit maximization," and "marginal revenue product" when applied to college athletics. Does our analysis of the NCAA imply that we view college sports as a mirror image of professional sports? Do the Clemson Tigers operate identically to the Chicago Bears?

The answer is no. College athletics are unique in many ways. The following chapters bring much of this uniqueness to light. A list of these aspects would include the following. (1) The mixture of athletic and academic production found among NCAA members does not exist in professional sports. Administrators sometimes face trade-offs between these two types of

8. See *NCAA News*, May 30, 1990, pp. 4–5.

production which are interesting. (2) There is a built-in demand for athletics among many students and alumni. The feeling of alumni and students that "their" team has succeeded or failed is sometimes stronger than that feeling among fans of professional teams. (3) The rules of NCAA contests generate a differentiated product from professional sports, which leads to the unusual occurrence that, in spite of clear inferiority in talent and performance skills, the college game can appeal to many people besides just students and alums much more than does the professional game.

In spite of these and other unique facets of college sports, approaching the NCAA and its members as economic entities remains warranted. In most cases, the peculiar aspects of college athletics change only the relevant variable to consider and not the appropriate analytical framework. For instance, professional sports are a for-profit venture. The typical assumption of profit maximization is normally appropriate here. In contrast, college sports operate in a nonprofit world. Does this require a noneconomic approach to understanding their behavior? No, because revenue is still an important objective to collegiate decision-makers. The difference with professional sports in this regard lies mainly in the form that net revenues take on the balance sheet. Instead of being clearly listed as dividends to stockholders or retained earnings, NCAA member surpluses end up in expense items such as salaries, equipment, buildings, or even transfers to the general fund. Similarly, college athletes do not produce revenues for which they receive an explicit wage or salary. Instead, they receive an in-kind payment from schools. Additionally, they provide implicit value to schools even if this value gets allocated to some other budgetary unit.

In sum, although almost every industry contains industry-specific qualities, a completely different analytical approach is not required for every case. The NCAA's unique qualities do not require a different kind of economic analysis, only careful application of the appropriate and existing analysis.

The NCAA in Law

This book does not attempt to discuss the subtleties of the application of state and federal laws to the NCAA. This topic could require an entire volume in itself, given the expansion of litigation in recent years concerning the NCAA. Existing references to the legal status of the NCAA and its members primarily relate to the antitrust aspects of NCAA activities. While reminding the reader of the dynamic nature of this topic and some unsettled issues, we can quickly describe the antitrust status of the NCAA today.

Application of antitrust laws to the NCAA is to a certain degree schizophrenic. On the one hand, on issues concerning the delivery of the NCAA's products, the courts have viewed the NCAA as any other industry. In the *National Collegiate Athletic Association v. Board of Regents of the University of Oklahoma et al.*, the U.S. Supreme Court found the NCAA to be a group of producers colluding to restrict television output in violation of the Sherman Act. In recent months, the Federal Trade Commission has filed an administrative complaint in federal court against the College Football Association (CFA) for alleged restrictive practices in its football television contract. On the other hand, when the issues before the courts have dealt with matters on the input side, such as personnel matters, antitrust enforcement and the courts have been lenient. The courts have generally viewed the NCAA's actions in this realm as voluntary agreements not subject to antitrust enforcement or due process. The case of the *NCAA v. Tarkanian*, in which the basketball coach at the University of Nevada at Las Vegas claimed that the sanctions the NCAA had placed on him violated due process, was denied. The U.S. Supreme Court, in a split decision, found that the NCAA was a voluntary organization not subject to due process provisions in spite of the involvement of a state universities. In its opinion in the Oklahoma case, the Court viewed, though did not necessarily endorse, the input restrictions as necessary for competitive balance and academic purposes. Thus, the NCAA's behavior in output markets has been monitored carefully by antitrust authorities, while its behavior in input markets has been basically untouched by antitrust.

3. Conclusion

The issues discussed in this chapter provide a snapshot of the questions addressed in this book. An entire volume could probably be filled solely with anecdotes related to the cartel interpretation of the NCAA. This, however, would take the book away from its main purpose. There already exist an ample number of stories about NCAA problems, especially recruiting violations, and NCAA inequities in enforcement. The purpose of this book is to provide a framework which will help to explain many of these specific episodes in more general terms.

T W O

Economic Theory
and the NCAA

T his chapter brings economic theory to bear on various
aspects of NCAA behavior. In section 1, the production of
certain public goods by the NCAA is considered. These public
goods include such activities as the standardization of the rules
of play, the provision of referees, and record keeping. In section 2, the economic theory of cartels is applied to NCAA behavior. The process of cartelization is examined with respect to
output (e.g., televised games) and input (players). In other
words, the behavior of the NCAA as a monopolist and a
monopsonist is analyzed. In section 3, the economic theory of
rent seeking is shown to be relevant to NCAA behavior. The
purpose here is to analyze the competition among member
schools for cartel rents. In section 4, the critical process of cartel
enforcement is discussed, the point being to study which
schools are put on probation by the NCAA and why. Some
summary remarks are offered in section 5.

1. The NCAA's Provision of Public Goods

Coalitions among producers are not formed without good reasons. The obvious motivation is increased firm wealth. However, either relatively low potential profits from collusion or the
enforcement of legal prohibitions on collusion may limit such
coalitions from emerging. The NCAA fits this model. Basically,
the low potential profits from collusion in intercollegiate sports
during the late 1800s meant that, if an association of schools
formed, some other motivating factor must have been present.

An alternative organizing incentive appears when producers face a common externality problem. Such an externality may, in fact, arise due to the activities of the firms in an industry. With each firm imposing costs on the others without compensating them, the balance sheet of every producer is negatively impacted. The case of fishermen harvesting fish in a common fishery is a classic example of such a negative externality. Each producer harvests more than would be harvested if the resource carried a price or, what is the same thing, were owned by someone. Consequently, all producers in the industry suffer the effects of rapidly depleted stocks of fish.

College athletic producers faced such a situation in the late 1800s and early 1900s.[1] Violence during college football contests had reached alarming proportions (a large number of players were being killed) due largely to the absence of effective punishment of such behavior. No one school had an incentive to reduce such tactics, since other teams would continue to use them and win. In addition to violent play, football was still in a formative period as far as its basic playing rules were concerned. The roots of rugby lingered in some rules recognized by some teams. Lack of standardized rules helped to contribute to the violent play, as well as contributing to difficulties in other aspects of on-the-field performance.

In many cases, the parties involved not only recognize the costs imposed on each other by such externalities but also clearly see the source of the problem. Yet recognition of the problem is no guarantee of a solution. Each producer may find itself in the so-called prisoners' dilemma.[2] All producers may agree that a superior outcome exists if each producer will refrain from or limit the activity creating the externality. But without a formal agreement or means to punish the aberrant behavior, each producer continues to engage in it. If any one firm imposes constraints on itself, the problem on the whole

---

1. The relevant historical details are covered in chap. 3.
2. The "prisoners' dilemma" originated in a story told by mathematician A. W. Tucker. The choice given two prisoners (held in isolation from one another) is to confess or not to confess, and the structure of the punishment for each choice is such as to lead each prisoner to confess even though each would be better off if he did not confess, provided that his compatriot also did not confess.

continues, and the self-constrained firm loses profits relative to the other firms. The fishery example typifies the problem. Fishermen clearly recognize the rapid depletion of fish stocks. Also, they recognize that, if all or most of them would limit their harvest, the problem would be alleviated. Still, no single producer will find it in his interest to limit catches.

Colleges with football teams in the late 1800s understood the costs and the benefits of reducing violent play. In fact, a few schools chose, at least for short periods, to limit the use of violent tactics. With no comprehensive agreement and most schools continuing to pursue such tactics, the problem of violent play persisted. Moreover, injuries and deaths grew in spite of the increased awareness of the problem, facts which lowered the appeal of the game to fans and jeopardized its future.

A stable solution to such externality problems requires some agreement, either explicit or implicit, among firms. In addition, the agreement must provide for rewards for holding to the terms of the contract and punishments for breaching the contract. Even when the participants know how to solve a problem, reaching an agreement to do so may be difficult. Benefits to contracting may be large, but the costs may also be large. In general, the organization of an externality-reducing institution is not a simple process.[3]

Clearly, the benefit from contracting is the reduction of an externality. As the size of the externality increases, the benefit and likelihood of reaching agreement increases, holding the costs of contracting constant. The costs of agreement stem from two main sources. First, the time and effort involved in negotiating an agreement is costly. The number of producers involved influences the size of this cost; more producers mean higher costs. Second, an opportunity cost is entailed in agreeing to a contractual association with other firms. Each firm loses some degree of self-determination and freedom of choice. The length and complexity of the agreement is a factor in determining the size of this cost. As these contracting and opportunity costs increase, the likelihood of reaching agreement falls, when the benefits are held constant.

---

3. For more general treatments of the costs of organization and agreement, see Buchanan and Tullock (1962) and Olson (1965).

In the case of college athletics, this organizing calculus played an important role, as evidenced by the fact that the problem of violent play persisted long after it was recognized. The costs of organizing, negotiation costs, and the loss of some power of self-determination proved high enough to block the early emergence of a wide-ranging agreement. Small groups of schools floated into and out of associations, but a far-reaching agreement was not forthcoming until the early 1900s.

The tide turned because of changes in the benefits of organization. As noted, the externalities of violence and non-standardized play grew to prohibitive levels in the late 1800s and early 1900s. This increased the potential benefits of organization, while the costs remained relatively constant. The implicit cost-benefit calculus finally led to an agreement between schools and the birth of the predecessor of the ultimate NCAA.

2. Cartel Theory and the NCAA

Collusion and Profits

The initial reason for cooperation among producers often centers on solving a common externality problem. The resulting association may provide such public goods as measurements, standards, and the like. In this section the focus shifts to consider how such an association can evolve into an organization with a different purpose. The primary purpose may remain constant, that is, the management of potential externalities; yet the organizational format can turn from reducing externalities to increasing joint profits. This scenario has been referred to as the by-product theory of organization.

The initial or startup costs of an organization are often high. These fixed and quasi-fixed costs hinder the effective solution of externality problems. As stressed in the case of the NCAA, the extent of the initial costs is evidenced by the degree to which violent play and other problems were allowed to grow before they were addressed. In spite of these large startup costs, once an association is organized and such origination costs have been incurred, the continuing costs of association may be quite low. In other words, variable and marginal costs are low with respect to the fixed costs, and the association enjoys economies of scale. In addition, the costs of expanding the scope of the association to include additional areas may be quite low; the association may enjoy economies of scope. The factor behind such economies is that the association already has a management and decision-making apparatus in place. Once an association is organized, given that the initial organizational costs are borne, the marginal costs of agreeing to extend the scale and scope of the association are low.

The areas into which the association extends its grasp can vary. The firms and organizations may agree on additional rules and institutions to reduce other externalities. However, producers may also use the cooperative apparatus to behave like a cartel. Such behavior includes making price-fixing agreements, placing restrictions and quotas on the quantity of the product sold, colluding on the purchase of inputs, and so on. To paraphrase Adam Smith, producers seldom get together without the discussion turning to plots against consumers and input suppliers.

The NCAA is no exception to this general maxim. The colleges did not originally cooperate for cartel purposes. Instead, the association that became the NCAA bore the initial costs of organization in order to provide public goods. Very shortly thereafter, the discussion turned from the reduction of violence and on-the-field rule standardization to price and output restrictions and restrictions on the purchase of inputs. For the most part, the evolution of the cartel took place over the first half of the 1900s. By 1950, these restrictions on college athletic product and resource markets had become the primary preoccupation of the NCAA.

The motivation behind market-restricting collusion by producers is easy to see. The rationale is to increase returns per firm relative to the situation in which firms freely compete with one another. This holds true whether the restrictions are in output or input markets. The fact that the NCAA is a nonprofit organization simply changes the balance sheet item which is maximized. Instead of "profits" or returns to shareholders, it may be implicit subsidies to the university general operating expenses, coaches' salaries, office facilities, and so on which are maximized. The accounting practices of colleges and universities merely mask the recipients of cartel rents.

Cartel Basics

The effects of cartel practices on profits have been well documented.[4] In the product market in an industry, if each firm prices its product competitively, the price charged by each firm will be driven toward its marginal cost. Over time, producers will reap only average or normal rates of return on their invested capital and the value of their time. As long as the firms' products are relatively interchangeable, increasing price above cost is not a profitable strategy. Collusion among producers to raise prices and restrict the quantity sold alters this outcome. Market and the individual firms' prices rise above costs, and profits per firm increase. Of course, the firms must effectively restrict prices and quantities to their agreed upon levels, or competition will return price and quantities to their competitive levels. This usually requires an enforcement or punishment procedure for noncompliance. Also, resource availability or some other factor must limit the entry of new competitors. As a general principle, a cartel will be more profitable the less responsive consumers are to price increases. Lack of an enforcement or punishment process, rapid entry into the marketplace of firms outside the cartel, or large consumer responses to price increases signal difficulties for cartel stability.

Likewise, in the market for inputs, if each firm competes for resources independently of other producers, each firm will have to purchase the resources at close to their marginal value to the firm, that is, their marginal revenue product. In contrast, collusion among firms in the purchase of resources changes this outcome. If firms agree to fix prices for inputs, the productive factors will be paid less than their MRPs. This difference between payment to the input and its MRP accrues to the firm.[5] In general, the conditions required for successful input collusion are also required for output collusion—an effective enforcement or punishment mechanism for noncompliance, a

---

4. For an intermediate-level discussion of cartel fundamentals, see Browning and Browning (1989). For more advanced treatments, see Stigler (1964), Osborne (1974), Asch and Seneca (1975), Green and Porter (1984), Waterson (1984), McGee (1988), and Shughart (1990).

5. Scully (1974, 1989) provides his view of how this process applies to Major League baseball.

limitation (for whatever reason) on alternative competition for inputs, and an input whose supply is relatively unresponsive to changes in its compensation. If any of the three conditions is absent, the profitability and stability of the collusive input agreement are threatened.

The NCAA has engaged in both types of market restraints. In the product market the NCAA's primary means of restricting output for many years was to specify the number of games that could be televised. Member schools signed a single contract to govern their revenues from televised games as well as the number of appearances their team could make over a season. These restrictions helped to increase revenues relative to the situation in which each school or group of schools would sign individual TV contracts (in fact, the NCAA itself made this claim). Additionally, the NCAA limited season length, although this could arguably be construed as the provision of a standardized format for competition. In the input market NCAA restrictions are far more numerous. Prohibitions on direct player payments—as well as in-kind and/or implicit favors, limitations on grants-in-aid, standardized scholastic requirements, and many other similar restrictions—exist. Although enacted in the name of standardized rules, most of these restrictions help to keep compensation to players below their MRPs and redistribute rents toward schools, athletic departments, and coaches.

Market Conditions and Cartels

The profitability of a cartel depends on overall supply and demand conditions in its markets. And, of course, market conditions change over time, and, thus, the benefits of collusion change. Whenever product demand increases, other things equal, the cartel becomes more profitable. It can obtain higher prices from consumers with the same level of costs. Increased profitability impacts on a cartel in various ways. For one, it can alter the prospects for the stability of the cartel. This is discussed in section 4 below. Also, if a competitive fringe of non-cartel producers is present in the market, higher profits mean higher potential benefits to cartel membership, and some of these firms will attempt to join the cartel. Increases in market demand for the product influences input market conditions;

specifically, the marginal value of inputs will increase, at least, on average. If producers hold input compensation steady, more rent will accrue to producers as product market demand and the marginal value of inputs increase.

Changes in market supply conditions are also important. Increases in overall market supply represent a threat to a cartel. New entry into the market by noncartel members or increases in production by cartel members above allotted quantities render the market more competitive. Other things equal, prices and profits will fall under these conditions. Additionally, an increase in market supply will encourage membership expansion by the cartel in order to bring some of the new production under the umbrella of cartel quantity restrictions. This helps the cartel maintain stability relative to outside competitors; however, per-firm profitability in the cartel falls, which may decrease internal stability.

All of these changes have affected the development of the NCAA. First, the demand for college athletics, especially football and basketball, has grown over the entire century. Growth of revenues and surpluses (correctly measured) make this clear. As a result, more and more of the "competitive fringe" schools have sought membership in the NCAA. Second, the supply of college athletics in terms of major participants has increased. This has prompted the NCAA to add members and, as discussed in the next section, has created friction within the NCAA. Third, while the demand for NCAA products has increased, the allowable compensation to athletes has remained almost constant (at least in real terms). This increase implies an increase in the rents accruing to other factors. This is seen most readily in the rise in coaches' salaries, athletic department expenditures, and university revenues from athletics.

As for the conditions necessary for successful and stable cartels (an enforcement and punishment mechanism, limited entry, and an inelastic supply of inputs), the NCAA has developed institutions to handle some of these problems and has benefited from underlying market conditions on others. Around 1950, the NCAA solved the problem of an effective enforcement and punishment mechanism by creating the Committee on Infractions. In addition, the sanctions for violations were radically strengthened in the 1980s (e.g., the adoption of the so-called death penalty for repeat offenders). Although entry of individual schools into the major college sports market has taken place, the NCAA itself enjoys a natural barrier to outside competition. This is due to the "lumpiness" of entry into the relevant market. In order to compete effectively with the NCAA, a school must not only break with the organization but also convince enough other major producers to exit so that a viable schedule of opponents is possible. Finally, the NCAA has also benefited from the inelastic supply of athletes. Most eligible athletes range from eighteen to twenty-two years of age and have relatively meager alternative opportunities.

3. Competition among Producers

Competitive Strategies

Cartel agreements, whether in output or input markets, typically restrict price competition and limit production. The intent behind these restraints is to create above-average profits in the output markets and a flow of economic rents from certain inputs which are compensated below their market value in input markets.

The cessation of explicit price competition, though, does not imply the disappearance of all forms of competition among producers. Profits at the firm level still remain a motivating force for individual members of the cartel. Moreover, as the cartel becomes more successful at extracting profits and rents, the potential gains from successfully out-competing rival producers increase. One would expect the level of nonprice competition to intensify as profit opportunities increase. Clearly, this creates a source of potential instability for any cartel.

Some forms taken by these alternative competitive strategies are easy to identify (from an analytical and not a cartel standpoint). The first is actual price competition. Firms may offer consumers secret price cuts or inputs above cartel wage inducements. If the goods or inputs are not traded in a single or a few central markets, such violations of the cartel agreement may not be easy to detect. On top of secret payments and price cutting, rival firms within a cartel may engage in competitive activities which deal on margins other than nominal prices. For example, the quality of the product offered to consumers may be altered. During the period of price regulation in the airline and banking industries, airlines competed by offering various attractions to customers such as brightly colored planes and scantily clad attendants, while banks built fancier facades, more expansive message boards, and plush facilities. In input markets, rival producers can also compete in terms of quality. They may offer different amenity and benefit packages to workers. In addition to these standard forms of nonprice (implicit) competition, the entrepreneurial spirit can lead firms to discover new ways to attract customers or inputs.

The NCAA has experienced such competition. The market restraints which have helped to create large surpluses and rents also create an atmosphere of intense competition for such rewards. Competition thrives in the NCAA both in terms of violations of its rules and in areas not covered by the rules. Recorded accounts as well as rumors of monetary and in-kind payments (e.g., cars) to recruits are numerous. The competition for prize recruits does not end with cash payments and free cars. Schools compete for athletes in areas not covered by the NCAA rules. These areas include physical capital such as training and practice facilities, stadiums and arenas, and living quarters. In addition, personal services, such as orientation and registration aid, tutoring, and special food, are offered in some cases. Also, firms expend resources to exploit their brand names in athletics and academics in order to attract athletes.

Importance of Alternative Competition

The competitive tools utilized by rival members of cartels, while often appearing frivolous and fanciful, ultimately play a crucial role. They determine each member's actual share of the cartel profits. The firms most skillful at circumventing the rules receive larger shares of cartel rents. This holds whether the circumvention occurs by means of a school making secret payments to athletes or by means of innovating new amenities and packaging of the amenities most desired by consumers or student athletes.

Circumvention of the NCAA agreement obviously occurs, and profits are unevenly distributed within the NCAA because of this competition. Cash inducements to athletes and explicitly prohibited in-kind benefits are offered. The latter range from cars to cosigned loans, phony jobs, airline tickets, T-shirts, and so on. Seemingly, these prohibited enticements occur frequently; yet, in spite of the frequency, the amounts involved are usually quite small relative to athletic revenues. Apparently, the enforcement process does retard the level of cash and in-kind payments.

In contrast, competitive expenditures to attract athletes and consumers not prohibited by the NCAA are quite large. Physical capital expenditures stand out among all others. Schools build elaborate stadiums, scoreboards, sky boxes, locker rooms, training facilities, and athletic dormitories, as well as stocking them with expensive furnishings and equipment. Also, expenditures which exploit school brand-name capital are growing. These include such items as brochures, videos, logos, advertisements, and specialized athletic department personnel, including coaches with well-developed public relations skills.

Even the most casual observation confirms the importance of these brand-name and physical capital expenditures in determining the final distribution of revenues among NCAA members. The schools with the most plush and spacious facilities, the smoothest recruiters, and the most successful programs dominate on the playing field, television appearances, alumni dollars, and, ultimately, cartel returns.

The alternative forms of competition not only redistribute revenues in a cartel but also provide a potential destabilizing force. As each firm seeks a larger share of rents, some firms will succeed; some will not. The losers have an incentive to intensify their competition and also to reconsider their membership in the cartel. In the extreme, membership no longer makes sense if a firm's share of the rents falls below the competitive level. Cartel stability requires at least some sharing of the benefits among members. On the other hand, sharing diminishes the rewards from expenditures to out-compete one's rivals.

The distribution of profits and the dynamics of cartel stability help to determine who will control the legislative and enforcement agendas of the cartel. The firms responsible for generating the lion's share of revenues hold the upper hand in this context. If they leave the cartel or balk at the redistribution of revenues, cartel stability faces a greater threat than if small-revenue firms leave. So whatever determines the distribution of revenues will also play a large role in determining the capture of the legislative and enforcement apparatus. Of course, the process is more complicated than that. Strategic behavior and coalition formation can occur; still, the powerful position of the cartel bulwark firms will provide a benchmark for control of the cartel.[6]

Naturally, the NCAA faces the same destabilizing influences from competition among members. The association constantly finds itself facing the issue of how to slice the pie. The first half of the century saw the smaller schools capture more and more of the revenues. This occurred by growth in membership and by restraints such as those on the number of television appearances a school could make. Beginning about 1980, though, some of the larger producers began asserting themselves. The division of the NCAA into separate competitive leagues, especially the IA/IAA split between major and smaller schools in football, was such an adjustment. More recently, the opposition by Oklahoma and Georgia to the single television package and Notre Dame's move, signing its own five-year television package worth $36 million, fall into this exercise of power by the larger schools.

The capture of the legislative and enforcement process by certain firms has also occurred in the NCAA. Again, the most successful programs, those with the largest physical and brand-name capital bases, have an advantage in this respect. In chapter 7, a specific hypothesis based on this proposition is tested. Also, whatever group is successful in dominating the legislative and enforcement process, it is clear that rivalry and self-interest will be apparent among schools when new issues and proposals arise. Many of the proposals will not benefit all schools, and support or opposition will center around the potential winners and losers from the proposals. In chapter 6,

6. "Strategic behavior" occurs when a firm, or in this case a school, alters the environment in which it competes so as to increase its profits. Examples of this type of behavior will be identified in chaps. 5, 6, and 7. For a general overview of strategic behavior in economics, see Rasmussen (1989) and Carlton and Perloff (1990).

the struggle over new athlete eligibility requirements, "Propositions 48 and 42," is used to portray this aspect of NCAA behavior.

Market Conditions and Intracartel Competition

Increases in product demand alter the returns from and the incentive to engage in circumvention of cartel rules. The higher profits implicit in higher product demand make cartelization more enticing. At the same time, they lure self-interested cartel members to intensify their efforts to obtain those profits because the reward to such competition is higher. This holds for both violations of the cartel agreement and nonprice forms of competition. The message here is that higher product demand is a double-edged sword for cartel stability. Over some periods, it may encourage cooperation toward collusive agreements. Over other periods and once agreements have been reached, it may encourage the destabilizing effects of intracartel rivalry.

Demand for college athletics has grown by leaps and bounds over this century as a whole and especially since about 1980. The new billion-dollar, multiyear basketball tournament contract with CBS testifies to this fact. The NCAA cartel has experienced both the benefits and costs of the higher profits from these increases in demand. Membership has increased, and new agreements have been reached. However, schools have intensified their efforts to obtain and increase their share of the spoils.

Another result of increases in demand for any cartel is that the marginal value of inputs will increase. If the cartel restricts compensation of some input, compensation rates and MRP for that input diverge further with an increase in demand. This development also has an up side and a down side for the cartel. The cartel or certain factors within the cartel reap higher rents at the expense of the restricted input. At the same time, each firm has a greater incentive to make more illicit inducements to the restricted input and to spend more on amenities which are attractive to the input.

The NCAA squarely faces this problem. As demand for college athletics has increased, player compensation in real terms has remained nearly constant. This provides schools and certain inputs, such as coaches and athletic personnel, with higher rents. These rents take the form of salaries, plush offices, and the like. However, the NCAA has also seen the problem of secret cash and in-kind payments multiply as well as the dissipation of rents into nonregulated physical amenities for athletes. In response, the NCAA has increased enforcement efforts and punishments. Also, steps have been taken to "cut costs" which, in most cases, means limiting the dissipation of the rents. Still, while raising the costs for offering secret enticements, the differential between the MRPs of athletes and their relevant compensation remains and grows. As long as this condition holds and the probability of catching violators is less than one, boosters and athletic personnel will continue to engage in the secret activity. And, if the NCAA does become more effective in enforcement, more dissipation of nonregulated amenities can be expected.

As discussed earlier, an inelastic supply of the restricted input enhances a cartel's ability to limit compensation and receive rents. An additional factor is the competitive nature of the supply of the input. If collusion among labor takes place, the firms in the cartel are no longer able to purchase from a competitive pool of labor. Instead, the input behaves like a monopolist. If either the supply curve of the input becomes more responsive to changes in its compensation or the various input suppliers organize, the ability of the cartel to drive a wedge between compensation and MRP is reduced. There are some indications that such developments may be in store in college athletics over the course of the next several years.

To this point in time, the NCAA has been able to draw its labor supply from an inelastic and disorganized source. Over time, this may change. As in professional sports, players may become increasingly aware of their marginal values to the school and the divergence of their compensation from these values. College athletes, younger and less informed, have taken longer than their professional counterparts but arestarting to recognize the divergence of their value to a school from the value of their compensation.[7] Also, as foreign sports

7. A single student athlete may not have an incentive to organize against schools. As stated earlier, such an organizational initiative takes time and can

leagues and domestic minor leagues in football and basketball grow, college athletes have more opportunities. Both of these changes may signal difficulties for the NCAA over the longer term.

4. Cartel Enforcement

Now that some of the basic economic principles concerning cartel behavior and the NCAA have been discussed, the problem of cartel enforcement can be discussed. This topic has been saved for last because some of the foregoing analysis is important in understanding the nature of the enforcement process. This is especially true in the specific application to the NCAA.

A necessary condition for successful cartel operation is a viable enforcement and punishment mechanism. Yet the mechanism must be cost-efficient. It is on this point that a cartel faces a dilemma. Widespread cheating on the cartel agreement signals the end of the cartel, and such behavior must be controlled. However, if members of the cartel are locationally dispersed when selling their products and purchasing inputs, enforcement may be expensive.

In general, the cartel has two ways to determine if firms are violating the collusive agreement. First, it can monitor each member directly, that is, engage in constant surveillance of each firm's practices. Second, it can use probabilistic evidence to infer when a producer's behavior diverges from agreed-upon principles. Unless cartel members sell and purchase in centrally located and well-organized markets, direct surveillance is prohibitively costly. With dispersed firms, the cartel enforcement agency is not able to monitor all members directly.

Without direct monitoring, the enforcement agency must monitor imperfectly. A relatively inexpensive way to infer cheating is by use of a probabilistic model. If some statistics are available on firm performance (profits, revenues), probabilistic inferences can be drawn about behavior. The enforcement pro-

---

be expensive. By the time a "union" is organized, it is likely that the initial organizers will have graduated. Thus, these initial organizers would bear the costs of organization but not enjoy the benefits. Of course, as in other occupations, professionals at organizing such groups might defray some of these costs.

cess, at least in a stylized way, is not difficult to imagine. Suppose the enforcement agency uses an end-of-year performance statistic as its guide. It knows past historical performance and from this can compute the probability of various levels of firm performance relative to the cartel as a whole. Using some decision rule, the enforcement agency infers a violation has occurred if firm-level performance exceeds its average performance relative to the cartel by a large amount; that is, the probability of such an outcome occurring by random chance is small. One would expect to see enforcement and punishment actions brought against members performing extraordinarily well given their historical performance.

Application of this analysis to NCAA enforcement is direct. Consider the rules regarding compensation to athletes. Given the number and location of schools and the diversity of places visited by schools in recruiting, direct surveillance is not possible. This is especially true in view of the limited enforcement staff of the NCAA but would still hold for even a much larger NCAA staff. The number of possible contacts between schools, athletes, coaches, and alumni is far too large for a cost-efficient system of direct surveillance monitoring. As a result, the NCAA uses probabilistic evidence to infer violations (at least at the initial stages of an investigation). The most obvious statistic from which to draw inferences is on-the-field performance. If a team's on-the-field performance increases dramatically relative to its historical average, illegal activity may be occurring. This idea is developed and tested further in chapter 5.

Enforcement has interesting implications for the allocation of rents within the NCAA. If the enforcement process is relatively successful at keeping compensation to athletes close to its agreed-upon value, such secret cash and in-kind payments will have little impact on the distribution of rents in the cartel. Instead, the allocation of rent to a particular school will depend primarily upon that school's ability to compete in the nonregulated areas. As we have seen already, these areas are largely physical and brand-name capital expenditures. Generally, traditional winners with a large stock of brand-name capital and schools with the financial resources to build up their physical capital stock will gain from the enforcement process. These programs have a built-in group of fans, large stadiums, and plush facilities and are therefore in a natural economic position to benefit from good teams, high rankings, conference championships, and bowl games.

5. Summary

This chapter develops a framework of the economic theory of cartels with which to explain and predict NCAA behavior. Some of the finer and more technical theoretical issues have been neglected in favor of seeking to provide a sense of the connection of various parts of the theory with the NCAA and its workings. Before moving on, some of the most important points from the preceding sections are summarized.

1. Cartels often originally organize to solve genuine economic problems. In the case of the NCAA, its original organizational purpose was to solve an externality problem, especially the problem of standardized rules and violent play.
2. Once organized, for whatever reason, firms often find the rewards of restraining output and input markets high, while the costs of reaching such agreements are low. The NCAA moved from on-the-field rules standardization and enforcement to collusive product and input market agreements.
3. Profits are the prime motive behind cartel actions. The NCAA has consistently adopted rules intended to enhance member revenues and profits (properly measured). These rules include the restraints on televised appearances as well as the restrictions on the eligibility and compensation of athletes.
4. Increases in demand for a cartel's product encourage more firms to join the cartel. Over this century more universities have undertaken athletic programs and NCAA membership has grown rapidly.
5. Successful input market cartels require a relatively inelastic supply of labor. Young athletes, the NCAA's primary input, have few alternative opportunities and to date are unorganized.
6. Increases in demand imply higher profits and more rent from restricted inputs. Over the century, NCAA revenues have grown rapidly, especially since about 1970. Over the

same period, athlete compensation has remained nearly constant in real terms.

7. Long-term success by a cartel requires barriers to new entry and competition. The NCAA has benefited from the "lumpiness" of entry into the organization of college athletics, that is, the need for many firms to agree to compete before a viable season for an alternative league can be scheduled. Also, recent state legislative restrictions on agents and alumni have given legal force to some NCAA restraints.

8. Higher cartel-wide profits encourage more intracartel rivalry. The years since 1970 have seen a breakdown of the NCAA television package, formation of Division IA/IAA, formation of the CFA, and the signing of an individual network television package by Notre Dame.

9. Much of the intracartel competition takes place in unregulated activities. While prohibited payments to athletes are made, the size of these expenditures is dwarfed by expenditures on physical and brand-name capital by member schools.

10. Cartel enforcement will most often proceed by the use of probabilistic evidence. The NCAA does not have a large enough staff for direct surveillance. Even with a larger staff, direct surveillance would be prohibitively costly. Therefore, the NCAA must rely on probabilistic evidence, such as on-the-field performance, to detect cheating on its rules.

11. The legislative and enforcement mechanism in a cartel will tend to be captured by the largest revenue producers. It seems apparent that some of the perennial winners and largest programs have successfully dominated the NCAA's internal processes.

12. Rivalry and firm self-interest will be apparent in struggles over newly proposed areas of collusion. In the NCAA, self-interest among schools is displayed in debates over such new issues as Propositions 48 and 42.

THREE

A Synoptic History
of the NCAA

With an analytical framework in hand, a more detailed history of the NCAA can be presented. However, the point of this chapter is not to provide a complete history of the NCAA. Other authors have provided this kind of comprehensive account.[1] Instead, this chapter reviews the most significant actions taken by the NCAA relating to its founding and evolution into a cartel. Each section views a historical period through the lens of cartel theory as presented in the previous chapter. Whereas that chapter emphasized analytics and minimized historical application, this chapter does just the opposite—it brings the history to the forefront while keeping the theory in the background.

The narrative presented here is not complicated. In economic terms football faced a growing externality problem at the turn of the century: the proliferation of violence and injury as well as the increasing use of nonstandardized rules on the playing field. The magnitude of this negative externality prompted college football powers to organize the body that would become the NCAA. Almost immediately, though, the young organization turned from the business of internalizing externalities to the business of cartelizing intercollegiate football. The evolution of the NCAA from a rule-making group into a trade-restraining cartel is apparent and explicable. The byproduct theory of collective action from the preceding chapter

1. The primary histories of the NCAA include Stagg (1946), Flath (1963), Lewis (1969), Falla (1981), and Lawrence (1982, 1987), as the well as *NCAA Proceedings* for various years.

provides the explanation. Once the costs of organizing the rule-making group were incurred, the additional costs to the schools of cartelizing such activities as recruiting, financial aid, and the number of games played were relatively low. Not surprisingly, the NCAA seized the opportunity to expand its scope. The history of the NCAA from the 1920s onward encompasses one attempt after another to build an output- and input-restraining organization to operate college athletics. For the most part, after 1950 these attempts were solidified and were quite successful.

Two points implicit in the preceding chapter are worth noting at the outset. First, the college football cartel did not manifest itself overnight but evolved in a series of graduated steps. The organization blossomed into a mature cartel between 1948 and 1952. The so-called Sanity Code of 1948, restricting financial aid to student athletes, and the 1951 restrictions on televising football games signaled the beginning of an era in which the NCAA aggressively pursued monopolistic and monopsonistic policies. Also, at this time the NCAA put into place the skeleton of an organizational structure to enforce the cartel agreement among schools. As will be shown, this was an important ingredient previously missing from the NCAA arsenal to dissuade schools from cheating on the cartel agreement. During the modern era, the association has expanded its control over individual athletic programs. Second, as in any cartel, member schools do not benefit equally from every new restraint and different participants (school presidents, athletic directors, coaches, and players) are not equally affected by cartel decisions. This is an important point to remember because the application of cartel theory to NCAA history does not imply that all of the participants in the NCAA equally benefit from or agree with all the rules. The facts of majority rule, restricted entry conditions, and inelastic factor supplies pressure some members and participants into submitting to some NCAA decisions even though they do not gain anything by doing so. It is therefore clear that there will be dissidents in the NCAA.[2]

2. This point is raised because of the misperception that any dissent suggests prima facie evidence that a cartel does not exist. Cartels face many prob-

Sections 1 and 2 of this chapter explore the pre-NCAA era and the emergence of the NCAA as an organization to control violence and standardize rules. Section 3 covers some of the early history of attempts by schools to collude (1905–45). Section 4 details the watershed years, 1946–53, when the NCAA blossomed into an effective cartel. Sections 5 and 6 list some of the output and input restraints adopted in the 1950s, 1960s, and 1970s. Section 7 singles out and examines the judicial controversy over the single television plan for football. Section 8 considers some of the more recent trends (the 1980s and 1990s). Section 9 concludes.

1. Early Attempts to Control Violence

Until the late 1870s, most collegiate sports were organized by students in athletic clubs.[3] Games were marked by violence, rough play, haphazard rules, and controversy over eligibility requirements. Athletes moved from school to school with no loss of eligibility, and club members hired professional athletes to participate in intercollegiate events. Against this backdrop, organizational initiatives began to emerge.

During the same period, football rules were a collection of soccer, rugby, and modern football rules. No standardized set of rules prevailed across teams. In 1873, representatives from Columbia, Princeton, Rutgers, and Yale met to decide on a set of general rules for football, soccer, and rugby. The group agreed to adhere to the rules of soccer for their football games. Harvard, a major force at that time in college football, decided to continue to follow rugby rules but subsequently found it difficult to schedule opponents (Falla 1981, pp. 6–7).

Over the remainder of the century several groups made unsuccessful attempts to standardize and regulate college football rules. In 1876, a meeting took place among Columbia, Harvard, Princeton, and Yale to decide on rules for college athletic

lems which can lead to dissent, not the least of which is the distribution of cartel rents in the face of interfirm differences in demand and costs as discussed in chap. 2. The costs of exit are also relevant to dissent.

3. See Baker (1982) and Goff, Shughart, and Tollison (1988) for a broader discussion of the development of amateur rules as barriers to entry in athletic competition in the late nineteenth and early twentieth centuries.

events, especially football. Yale balked at the majority's decision to allow only eleven players on the field for each team. The amendment passed nonetheless, and the other three schools formed the first football rules committee, calling itself the Intercollegiate Football Association (IFA). The IFA regulated the rules of college football, although little was done to control violence on the playing field. As a result, the IFA's efforts were short-lived. By 1894, only Princeton and Yale remained in the IFA, and the organization was virtually powerless. The University Athletic Club of New York formed a new football rules committee in that same year, but this group also failed to stem the tide of violence on the playing field (Falla 1981, pp. 8–11; Lawrence 1982, pp. 26–30; Stagg 1946, pp. 18–20).

The Intercollegiate Conference of Faculty Representatives (the Big Ten) formed in 1895 and introduced faculty control of college athletics to promulgate regulations pertaining to eligibility and amateurism. The conference took steps toward limiting entry. Its rules outlawed participation in a collegiate sport by persons who had taken part in any athletic contest in which money prizes were offered (Chu, Segrave, and Becker 1985, p. 7; Savage et al. 1929, p. 41). The same year, the large schools in the East formed the new Football Rules Committee and asked Amos Alonzo Stagg of the Big Ten to join the proceedings. These rules committees and conferences, along with a number of other college athletic committees, did not quell the level of violence in intercollegiate sports. In the case of the Football Rules Committee, the unanimity principle of decision making posed a stumbling block. To pass a new rule or to change an existing rule, all participants had to agree. One dissenter could thus block any proposed rule change (Stagg 1946, pp. 21–22). Schools which benefited from violent tactics on the field used their bargaining power under the unanimity rule to overturn any rule change that would adversely affect their ability to use these techniques. Accordingly, the rules committee made few decisions of consequence and accomplished little to control brutality and violent play.

2. The Birth of the NCAA

The problem of violent play grew to such proportions that President Theodore Roosevelt took an interest. In 1905 alone, eighteen deaths and 159 serious injuries occurred in college football. On October 9, 1905, Roosevelt called together representatives from Harvard, Princeton, and Yale to discuss solutions to the problem of violence in college football by means of enforcement of the current rules or the creation of new rules to enhance safety. Little came from this meeting, except that those present acknowledged that the primary problems with intercollegiate football were violence and disregard for the hodgepodge of existing rules (Flath 1963, p. 46; Lewis 1969, p. 70). Moreover, the sport was suffering more generally. After the 1905 season, Columbia abolished its football program; Northwestern suspended play for a year; and California and Stanford scrapped football in favor of rugby.

Later the same year, Chancellor Henry MacCracken of New York University convened yet another conference of thirteen delegates from eastern schools with football teams to decide the following: "1) Should football be abandoned? 2) If not, what reforms are necessary to eliminate its objectionable features? 3) If so, what substitute would you suggest to take its place?" (*New York Times*, December 8, 1905, p. 9). By a two-thirds majority, the conference delegates decided not to abolish football but to reform the sport. The delegates also resolved to meet later in the month to form a new rules committee to solve the problem of violent play.

On December 28, 1905, a much larger contingent of sixty-two schools sent delegates to the second conference. Notable absentees were the major schools that made up the old Football Rules Committee. The delegates participating in the second conference voted to form a new athletic association. To this end, they set up an executive committee to write a constitution and to form a permanent sports association. Thus, the Intercollegiate Athletic Association of the United States (IAAUS) was founded, which in 1910 changed its name to the National Collegiate Athletic Association. The delegates also established a new rules committee and authorized it to attempt to align itself with the old Football Rules Committee, headed by Yale's Walter Camp (Flath 1963, p. 48; Falla 1981, p. 15).

The old and new committees met in New York in early January 1906 and agreed to a temporary alignment to make consistent rules. The members of the NCAA explicitly charged the new rules committee with "elimination of rough and brutal play . . . and making the rules definite and precise in all respects" (*New York Times*, December 29, 1905, p. 7). At the combined meeting of the two committees, the members dropped the need for unanimous consent in favor of requiring only a simple majority vote of the members for a rule change (Stagg 1946, p. 27). By the time of the first annual meeting of the NCAA in December 1906, thirty-eight schools had ratified its constitution. As a consequence of the high participation rate in the NCAA and its standardization of rules and outlawing of brutal play and violent techniques, the number of serious injuries in college football dropped over the next several years.

Let's quickly recapitulate these events through the eyes of economic theory. The NCAA formed in order to resolve an externality problem: violence and the lack of standard rules on the football field. With no single authority regulating the rules in football, a prisoners' dilemma developed. If all teams played by the rules, then any one school could benefit at the expense of its rivals by breaking the rules, using brutal and violent techniques to defeat opponents who adhered to the regulations of safe play. If all teams acted in this way, all schools would have an incentive to play rough and an inefficient amount of violence would prevail. The 1905 agreement resulted from the fact that the costs of diverse rules and excessively violent techniques of play had become greater than the benefits to individual schools. Without a uniform set of rules, confusion arose about the relevant rules when schools under the jurisdiction of different committees played one another. The public outcry about violence in 1905 that President Roosevelt was responding to threatened the very existence of collegiate football, as schools started to discontinue their programs.

The original mission of cooperation among schools focused on providing public goods: reducing violence and standardizing play. This is explicitly seen in the directive to the rules committee. While the NCAA initially organized as a public goods provider, it did not maintain this activity as its primary objective. The NCAA quickly turned its attention from standardizing rules to instituting the outlines of a cartel.

3. Early Restraints, 1905–46

At its first annual convention in 1906, the NCAA adopted a constitution which stated its broad purposes. While listing lofty goals and motivations, the document left ample room for the NCAA to expand from public-goods provider into cartel rules enforcer. Part of its stated purpose was "the regulation and supervision of college athletics throughout the United States, in order that the athletic activities in the colleges and universities may be maintained on an ethical plane in keeping with the dignity and high moral purpose of education" (*NCAA Proceedings* 1906, p. 29). While the statement appears innocuous enough, the NCAA almost immediately stepped beyond the simple "regulation and supervision" of on-the-field rules. Instead, maintaining college athletic activities on a high "ethical plane" soon meant eligibility rules, output restraints, and other cartel-like activities.

The new eligibility rules regulated many aspects of college athletics. They determined the allowable length of participation by student athletes; the limit was set at three years because a student had to sit out one year after admission or transfer. The restrictions also required student athletes to be full-time students. In conjunction with these basic eligibility rules, members adopted rules pertaining to the amateur status and financial remuneration of athletes. Inducements to influence student athletes to enter college were deemed illegal. Also, enticing students to stay in school through direct or indirect financial aid for the sole purpose of pursuing athletics was condemned (*NCAA Proceedings* 1906, pp. 33–35).

As mentioned, students formed and operated most extracurricular organizations prior to the inception of the NCAA. This soon changed. Faculty representatives and nonathletic representatives dominated the command structure of the NCAA. As Paul Stagg (1946, p. 48) remarked, "The association from the outset was a faculty body as distinct from an athletic body." Since these early days, administrators, faculty, and athletic administrators at various schools have wrestled with one another for primary control of athletics. It would be incorrect to view the participation of most schools as being dominated solely by athletic department wishes over the course of NCAA history.

An elected president, vice-president, secretary-treasurer, and Executive Committee constituted the upper-level management of the NCAA. The Executive Committee carried out the day-to-day operations of the new organization (Lawrence 1982, pp. 63–64).

The period between 1906 and 1920 was generally uneventful for the NCAA, although several trends were evident. For one, the NCAA extended its grasp beyond football. During the period eight more college sports besides football were put under the association's jurisdiction. Two new study groups were formed in 1913: the Committee to Study Methods of Athletic Regulation and Control in Other Countries and the Committee to Assist in the Adjustment of Athletic Differences between Colleges (Stagg 1946, p. 45; Falla 1981, p. 20). Early on, the NCAA had trouble forcing members to adhere to the regulations. Because of this difficulty, the NCAA passed a resolution in 1919 intended to encourage compliance with the rules of eligibility and amateurism.

> The association recommends that its members schedule games hereafter with those institutions only whose eligibility code is in general conformity with the principles advocated by this Association, such as the freshman eligibility, . . . the one year migratory rule, the limitation in the years of athletic participation and the amateur rule. (*NCAA Proceedings* 1919, p. 27)

From the NCAA's standpoint, the weakness in the resolution was that it only recommended adherence to these rules—the NCAA had not yet organized a regulatory mechanism to enforce the rules.

In 1920, college athletics and especially college football entered what some have called its "golden age." To a large extent, this refers to the dramatic growth in popularity experienced by college football between 1920 and 1950. Prior to 1920, interest already extended beyond campus borders; the 1920s, 1930s, and 1940s witnessed the expansion of college athletics from a small cottage industry into a nationwide preoccupation.

An obvious indication of NCAA growth over this period is the size of its membership. At its inception, the NCAA numbered fewer than 100 members. By 1924, it had grown to 135 members. By 1945, the NCAA boasted 210 members. In the early years, the group almost had to coax institutions into membership. By the 1920s, many schools were actively seeking membership.

The alterations in athletic facilities that were made over this period are one of the best indications of the large increase in actual fan interest that had occurred since the birth of the NCAA. Prior to 1920, most teams played in small stadiums much like or even smaller than those of many present NCAA Division III teams. Between 1920 and 1940 this situation changed radically as schools began to construct new, large-scale stadiums because of attendance growth. In the period 1920–40, over forty new football stadiums were constructed at current Division I-A schools. During the 1940s and 1950s, as the popularity of football soared, many of the original structures were expanded and new stadiums continued to be built. Perhaps the Big Ten experienced the most significant growth over this period. Table 1 presents data on new construction and expansion of Big Ten football stadiums between 1920 and 1950. While some of the original structures were relatively small by contemporary standards, by 1950 most of the Big Ten stadiums were within a few thousand seats of their current size. While demand and television audiences continued to grow after 1950, these schools experienced their largest increases in live attendance over the 1920–50 period.

TABLE 1
Stadium Construction for Selected Institutions

Institution	Year and Seating Capacity
Michigan	1927: 72,000* / 1949: 97,239 / 1956: 101,001
Wisconsin	1921: 29,783 / 1926: 38,239 / 1940: 45,000 / 1951: 51,000
Purdue	1924: 13,500* / 1949: 51,000
Iowa	1929: 53,000* / 1956: 60,000
Northwestern	1926: 45,000* / 1949: 49,256
Michigan State	1923: 14,000* / 1948: 51,000
Illinois	1923: $1,700,000**
Ohio State	1922: $1,341,000**

Sources: Football programs of various institutions reported above.
*Denotes construction of new facility.
**Denotes construction costs of new facility; capacity unavailable from source.

During the late 1920s and the 1930s the commercialization of college sports and inducements to athletes expanded. In fact, these aspects attracted the attention of organizations and writers not typically concerned with sports. For instance, in 1929 the Carnegie Foundation issued a report on abuses in college sports entitled *American College Athletics*. The report alleged and provided evidence of numerous NCAA rule violations, especially in the areas of the illegal recruitment and subsidization of athletes. About the same time, editorials appeared in the *New York Times* (November 7, 1930, and December 23, 1930) criticizing abuses in college sports, and more generally the disproportionate attention given sports on some college campuses. Several campus newspaper editors even voiced support for direct monetary payments to athletes for their services. The prominence of the attention given the abuses and commercialization within college sports provides a residual indication of the newfound popularity of college athletics over this period. Without a strong demand for the product, the "problems" of athlete subsidization and commercialization would not have surfaced. The widespread subsidization reported by the Carnegie Foundation adds to this evidence. If college athletics generated little interest across schools, secret payments and inducements to athletes would have been trivial or nonexistent in degree and scope.

Because of the growth in demand for college sports and the associated rules infractions, the NCAA took a renewed interest in the regulation of outputs and inputs over these years. Many of the regulations put into effect during the period bear the clear marks of cartelization as opposed to rules standardization. For example, in 1920 the association passed a regulation making athletes ineligible if they competed for any other athletic organization without permission. This rule applied even during vacation periods. By 1922, the NCAA had adopted a new ten-point code which defined eligibility more narrowly. The code disallowed participation by graduate students, competition against noncollege teams, and participation beyond three years. In addition, it asserted absolute faculty control over college sports programs (Falla 1981, p. 237).

Although NCAA restrictions continued to lack effective enforcement over this period, the association recognized the problem and took small steps to rectify it. In retrospect, these additional steps, by themselves, did not end the impotence of the NCAA regulations; yet they were precursors and necessary to the ultimate solution which was attained in the early 1950s. First, the NCAA openly promoted conference affiliation. Along with affiliation, the NCAA stressed conference-level regulation and enforcement. Second, at the 1940 convention, the NCAA added investigative and judicial functions to its legislative powers.

This period of NCAA history fits compactly into the theory developed in the previous chapter. By 1920, the NCAA had faced and overcome most of the initial organizational costs in order to overcome the problems of violence and nonstandard rules of play. In a manner reminiscent of the American Medical Association and the American Bar Association, the NCAA's attention was diverted beyond the bounds of quality certification and externality reduction to product and supply restrictions. Once members were meeting annually, the marginal costs of discussing input prices for athletes, eligibility rules, recruitment practices, and output restrictions were relatively low.

The growth in demand in the 1920–50 period fueled the interest in cartelization. With the initial organizational costs now borne, the explosion in demand meant increased revenues and rents to institutions and to the coaches, administrators, and faculty of those institutions. In addition to the direct revenue benefits, the indirect advantages from increased advertising, student enrollment, and the like spurred a desire for greater control over and maximization of these revenues. The benefits of successful sports programs were not lost on the administrators and faculty of that day. Besides establishing faculty and administrative control over athletics, institutions constructed new and greatly enlarged sports facilities. Even before this "golden age," faculty and administrators recognized the potential rewards to be reaped from college athletics. Woodrow Wilson, then president of Princeton, told alumni in 1890 that "Princeton is noted in this wide world for three things: football, baseball, and collegiate instruction" (*New York Times*, June 8, 1906, p. 58).[4]

4. In 1962, Robert Strozier, former dean of students at the University of Chicago, commented on the perception of the school held by others after it

In this initial cartel period, the NCAA relied on voluntary compliance with its regulations. But as is common in collusive arrangements, individual schools could improve their lot if they cheated while others held to the restrictions. Member schools in the aggregate would benefit from compliance but had an incentive not to comply while expecting noncompliance from others. The NCAA responded to this problem ineffectively. It adopted the "Ten-Point Code," stressed enforcement at the conference level, and took upon itself investigative and judicial powers. However, these measures did not have a practical organizational mechanism to make them work.

4. The Sanity Code and Its Aftermath

Up to this point, the NCAA had adopted many collusive restraints regarding eligibility and institutional behavior. The episodes of the 1920s, especially as detailed by the Carnegie report, highlighted the weaknesses of the rules. Institutions and athletes skirted the rules on a regular basis. The NCAA possessed rules but not the power to make them stick. In response, the NCAA made fledgling attempts in the 1920s and 1930s to remedy the situation. As noted, though, they succeeded only in strengthening the rules, not in enforcing them. In the years 1946–53, the NCAA made the transition from a loosely tied, mostly voluntary association to an effective cartel.

---

dropped football in 1939. He stated that top-rated students started attending less academically qualified schools that had football teams instead of the University of Chicago. "I believe that the resolution to return to football competition would say something which could not be said in any other fashion to the public, and something needs to be said" (Nelson 1962, p. 17).

A more recent example of the benefit a college can receive from a student athlete is the Auburn University football program. When Bo Jackson attended Auburn University between 1982 and 1985, season ticket sales increased from $41,000 to $61,000 per year. If an average ticket is $10 and there are five home games per year, this would have increased revenues to the school by $1 million. Auburn school officials also thought that at least some of the 1,700 increased applications per year (at $15 each) were attributable to Jackson.

McCormick and Tinsley (1988) have recently looked at the role of a successful athletic program in generating advertising for the school and attracting academically superior students. They conclude that schools with big-time athletic programs, ceteris paribus, attract freshmen with higher Scholastic Aptitude Test scores than other schools.

During July 1946, several collegiate conferences held a meeting in Chicago to discuss the practical aspects of trying to enjoin schools from cheating on NCAA rules. The conferences in attendance were the Big Ten, Pacific Coast, Southwest, and Southeastern. They drafted a document called "Principles of Conduct of Intercollegiate Athletics" and circulated it among NCAA members. At the 1948 convention, these principles were voted into the NCAA constitution and became known as the Sanity Code. The Sanity Code represented the first attempt by the NCAA to couple rules on amateurism, financial aid, and eligibility with an enforcement mechanism (Flath 1963, pp. 206–19).

Sections Four and Five of the Sanity Code, entitled "Principles Governing Financial Aids to Athletes" and "Principles Governing Recruiting," contained the most important parts of the code. Financial aid could only be given to student athletes through the normal channels that other students were compelled to follow. The Sanity Code restricted aid to include only tuition and fees, and required the terms of the financial agreement to be given to the student and published by the school. The code explicitly stated that financial aid be "awarded on the basis of qualifications of which athletic ability is not one." At least in theory the provisions banned financial aid for athletic ability; need and academic performance were the only justifiable reasons for such aid.

Section Five of the Sanity Code, "Principles Governing Recruiting," prohibited official representatives of the university from offering financial aid to potential student athletes on the basis of their athletic ability. The representatives of the university could describe the financial aid possibilities under Section Four of the code, but Section Five established the principle that the student athlete should be treated no differently from any other student in matters relating to financial aid. In effect, this regulation pushed all athletic scholarships through the regular financial aid routes. It did not actually restrict schools in practice from differentiating athletes and nonathletes, but it did provide the NCAA with more reliable data on aid that was given.

In contrast to previous attempts, the Sanity Code did not just initiate rules; it created an enforcement mechanism to handle violations. A three-member Compliance Committee became the final arbiter of the Sanity Code, with a Fact-Finding Committee serving as its investigative arm. The constitution bestowed upon the Compliance Committee the power to interpret legal and illegal practices. Only a two-thirds vote of NCAA members could overturn the Compliance Committee's decisions. A problem the committee quickly encountered was that the only form of punishment given to it by the NCAA constitution was the termination of an individual school's NCAA membership. The extremity of this punishment ultimately reduced its credibility and became the downfall of the code.

The sentiment in favor of the Sanity Code was in no way unanimous. Institutions from the South and Southwest were the most frequent dissenters. For instance, the athletic director of the University of Maryland questioned the fairness and equity of restricting competition on a direct, monetary scale. He argued that the older, more established schools, primarily in the North and East, possessed facilities and reputations to attract quality athletes while southern schools did not have such physical assets. His claim is borne out by the statistics from that era. The stadium sizes for several of the Big Ten schools around this period were quite large. By the early 1950s, almost every school possessed a facility with seating in excess of fifty thousand and the seating capacity of Michigan's stadium already approached one hundred thousand. In contrast, Tennessee, a southern institution, which in 1990 had the second largest stadium in college football, averaged an attendance of less than twenty-five thousand per game in 1950.[5] While a few southern schools, such as Louisiana State, already had grown into powerhouses, on average the southern schools lagged behind their northern counterparts in tradition, attendance, and interest in athletics before 1950.

Several schools publicly stated that they would not agree to the rules set down by the Sanity Code.[6] In spite of this opposition, the Compliance Committee, with the help of the Fact-Finding Committee, proceeded to investigate possible viola-

5. These data were obtained from Tennessee's football program.

6. See, for instance, Virginia's rebuttal discussed in *New York Times*, July 27, 1949, and, later, opposition by four university presidents (*New York Times*, April 28, 1953).

tors. The Compliance Committee found seven members in violation of the Sanity Code and asked for their termination from the NCAA (Boston College, University of Maryland, the Citadel, Villanova University, University of Virginia, Virginia Military Institute, and Virginia Polytechnic Institute). [7] In January 1950, the Council and Executive Committee terminated the seven schools. The final hurdle was to bring the termination of the seven accused schools to the floor of the convention for a vote. The vote for termination was 111 to 93, thus voting down the resolution because it lacked the two-thirds majority needed for passage. The arguments over the merits of the Sanity Code carried over to the next NCAA convention, held in 1951 (Falla 1981, p. 134; Lawrence 1982, pp. 154–59).

At its 1951 convention, the NCAA voted on an amendment to erase Section Four from the Sanity Code. This section outlined what financial aid entailed (tuition and fees) and who could administer the aid program. The Sanity Code officially lapsed when the members voted by a greater than two-thirds majority to repeal Section Four. The Compliance Committee now had no enforcement mechanism and became a useless institution (Lawrence 1982, pp. 167–68).

During 1951, the Council of the NCAA adopted a Twelve-Point Plan advising schools on how to diminish the negative opinion the public held of intercollegiate sports (*NCAA Proceedings* 1951, p. 106). The first three recommendations concerned reducing the number of practices held and games played. Points six through twelve told schools to reduce their costs by limiting financial aid. Points six through twelve also suggested limiting financial grants, discontinuing excessive entertainment for prospects, and eliminating excessive recruiting expenditures. The 1951 convention incorporated the Twelve-Point Plan into the constitution and agreed to propose new legislation pertaining to what financial aid was allowable. The legislation stated that "any college athlete who receives financial assistance other than that administered by his institution (tuition and fees) shall not be eligible for intercollegiate com-

7. In addition to these seven members, other schools in the South and the Southwest ran into trouble during the Sanity Code era. These include Kansas, Oklahoma A&M, and Missouri. At one time as many as twenty schools faced suspension (*New York Times*, May 29, 1949, section 5, p. 6).

petition" (*NCAA Proceedings* 1951, p. 254). In practice, this still channeled aid to athletes through general financial aid programs but allowed aid to be given as long as it was not based solely on athletic ability.

The NCAA officially disbanded the Compliance Committee in 1952 and in its place created a Membership Committee (and later in the year the Subcommittee on Infractions) as its enforcement mechanism. The Membership Committee enforced all NCAA academic and amateur standards. The Subcommittee on Infractions, the investigative arm of the Membership Committee, reported any violation of NCAA rules to the Membership Committee. The Membership Committee then made recommendations to the NCAA Council, which presented the suggested penalties for a particular violator to the full convention (Falla 1981, p. 136).

In 1953, the Council of the NCAA received the power to impose penalties that fell short of outright termination. This new flexibility gave the Council more credibility with respect to potential violators. In an equally important step, the Council was empowered to mete out penalties, without membership approval, between conventions. The entire convention would now act only as a final appellate group. The operational control of enforcement fell to the NCAA Council. At the 1954 convention, to streamline the enforcement process, the members centralized all investigative power in the renamed Committee on Infractions, whose membership included those already on the Council.

By restricting financial aid to student athletes through the Sanity Code, the NCAA members lowered the costs of one of their major inputs. The free market situation in which schools competed with one another for student athletes no longer existed. Schools were only allowed to pay student athletes a predetermined amount (tuition and fees), which lowered their total costs of operation. The arrangement also lowered search costs for the NCAA in finding rule violators by stipulating that all financial aid had to go through the financial aid office at the aid-giving school. The terms of financial aid were also to be published in an official publication of the school. The financial aid restrictions kept wages below market levels, and the centralization of records lowered the cost of detecting a violation of these rules.

Why did the NCAA overcome the enforcement hurdle at this particular time? The problem had persisted for decades, and the solution was not so complicated as to elude earlier generations of leaders. The answer resides in the underlying economic conditions. By agreeing on an enforcement mechanism, schools gave up more of their individual control over their programs. Schools gaining the most by breaking the rules had the most to lose. On the other side, by restricting input payments, the enforcement mechanism would benefit schools financially. Although college athletics had always enjoyed popularity, the 1920–50 period witnessed a boom in the demand for college sports. As the 1950s dawned, college sports began to tap the revenues from television exposure. As cartel theory suggests, the return to producers from collusion on inputs and outputs is greater as the demand for the final product grows. The demand growth for college sports over this period increased the benefits of an effective enforcement mechanism across institutions.

Also, what happened during this period falls in line with the predictions of the theory of the relative distribution of cartel rewards. While restricting payments to student athletes, the rules allowed athletic powers with existing physical and brand-name assets to capitalize on these assets. The schools with better facilities and academic and athletic reputations (usually in the North and the Midwest) had a distinct advantage over the schools with up-and-coming athletic and academic programs (usually in the South and the Southwest).

5. The NCAA Control of Output, 1950–70

The Sanity Code period and the eventual handling of the enforcement problem signaled a new era of regulation within the NCAA. With an enforcement mechanism near or in hand, the NCAA began to consider the regulation of outputs and inputs in increasing detail. In this section some of the NCAA restraints on output are reviewed.

With the rise of televised sports, output became an increasingly important area for NCAA regulation. The first order of business was to estimate the impact of televised games on college sports. In 1949, the NCAA spent $5,000 on a study of television and sports. By early 1951, the association had formed a permanent Television Committee. As part of this interest in television's impact, the National Opinion Research Center (NORC) conducted a statistical analysis of the relationship between television and live attendance at football games. NORC's study found that, during the 1949 and 1950 seasons, attendance fell by an average of 6 percent in areas where games were televised and increased by 2.5 percent in areas where they were not (Lawrence 1982, pp. 231–32).

Along with the study of television came new restrictions on its use. One of the first moves was to place a moratorium on universities' unilaterally agreeing to televise their football games during the 1951 season. The Television Committee restricted the total number of games televised in 1951 to twenty and the number of times any one school could appear to two (one home and one away game) (Falla 1981, p. 240). The control of total games and appearances per team continued into the 1980s. Those members who did not follow the Television Committee's rules would be declared a member not in good standing with the NCAA. When the University of Pennsylvania publicly refused to follow the committee's rules, it was assessed this penalty. As a result, several Ivy League schools declined to play Pennsylvania. This brought home a major cost of expulsion or sanction by the NCAA—a lack of opponents. With few opponents to play, Pennsylvania changed its decision and did not televise its games (Lawrence 1982, p. 244).

For 1952, the Television Committee, with the agreement of the membership, limited the total number of games that could be televised nationally to twelve. A network could not televise any other game without approval by the NCAA. Also, a restriction of one TV appearance per school was incorporated into the agreement. Including regional games and extra games agreed to by the NCAA, a total of thirty-three games were televised. The 1952 season is also the first year that the NCAA negotiated a national television network contract. NBC paid $1.15 million for the exclusive right to televise games during 1952 (Falla 1981, pp. 105–6).

During the following years, demand for college football continued to grow, as evidenced by the expansion of television revenues. Table 2 lists television revenues for the years 1952–83. Between 1955 and 1959, revenues paid to the NCAA by NBC

TABLE 2
NCAA Television Contracts, 1952–83

Years	Network	Amount	Years	Network	Amount
1952–53	NBC	$1,444,000	1964–65	NBC	7,800,000
1954	ABC	2,000,000	1966–69	ABC	10,200,000
1955	NBC	1,250,000	1970–71	ABC	12,000,000
1956	NBC	1,600,000	1972–73	ABC	13,500,000
1957	NBC	1,700,000	1974–75	ABC	16,000,000
1958	NBC	1,800,000	1976–77	ABC	18,000,000
1959	NBC	2,200,000	1978–79	ABC	29,000,000
1960	ABC	3,125,000	1980–81	ABC	31,000,000
1961	ABC	3,125,000	1982*	ABC/CBS	59,000,000
1962–63	CBS	5,100,000	1983*	ABC/CBS	64,000,000

Note: The compensation for the contracts stated the "minimum aggregate compensation to the participating NCAA member institutions" (see *NCAA v. Board of Regents of the University of Oklahoma*, p. 6). Also, when the contract was for more than one year, the money is per year.
Source: David Greenspan, "College Football's Biggest Fumble," pp. 34–35.
*Turner Broadcasting System, Inc. (TBS) for these years agreed to pay $17.7 million to televise NCAA games.

rose almost $1 million (to $2.2 million). In 1960, the NCAA switched its exclusive television contract from NBC to CBS. CBS paid the NCAA $6.25 million for the exclusive rights to televise college football games during the next two years (Greenspan 1988, pp. 34–35). In 1966, the NCAA ended the practice of competitive bidding for the television contract and instead dealt exclusively with ABC. For the 1972 and 1973 football seasons, fees paid to the NCAA by ABC amounted to $13.5 million per year, with $487,857 paid for each national telecast and $355,000 for regional appearances (Falla 1981, pp. 114–17). In spite of the increased television exposure and revenues, live attendance at college games continued to expand. Table 3 provides some data on this growth in live attendance.

The NCAA negotiated two-year contracts exclusively with ABC until 1977, when the NCAA adopted new "principles of negotiation." These new principles did not entail submission of new television contracts for agreement by all members but instead pursued long-term (four-year) exclusive contracts with ABC. During the first four-year contract with ABC, revenues to the NCAA and its members averaged $30 million per year. As

TABLE 3
Total College Football Attendance, 1948–89

Year	Attendance	Year	Attendance
1948	19,100,000	1969	27,600,000
1949	19,700,000	1970	29,500,000
1950	19,000,000	1971	30,500,000
1951	17,500,000	1972	30,800,000
1952	17,300,000	1973	31,300,000
1953	16,700,000	1974	31,200,000
1954	17,000,000	1975	31,700,000
1955	17,300,000	1976	32,000,000
1956	18,000,000	1977	32,900,000
1957	18,300,000	1978	34,300,000
1958	19,300,000	1979	35,000,000
1959	19,600,000	1980	35,500,000
1960	20,400,000	1981	35,800,000
1961	20,700,000	1982	36,538,637
1962	21,200,000	1983	36,301,877
1963	22,200,000	1984	36,652,179
1964	23,400,000	1985	36,312,022
1965	24,700,000	1986	36,387,905
1966	25,300,000	1987	36,462,671
1967	26,400,000	1988	35,581,790
1968	27,000,000	1989	36,406,297

Source: David Greenspan, "College Football's Biggest Fumble,"
pp. 64–65; and *NCAA News*, January 3, 1990, p. 16.

an example of how these fees were divided up during the 1980 season, each of the nationally televised games (twelve) earned a fee of $600,000 and each regional game (forty-six) earned $426,779.[8] Division I schools received a total of $27,842,185, or 89.9 percent of the total fees; Division II schools received $625,195, or 2.0 percent of the total fees; Division III schools received $385,195, or 1.3 percent of the fees; and the NCAA itself received $2,147,425, or 6.9 percent of the total fees (*National Collegiate Athletic Association v. Board of Regents of the University of Oklahoma et al.*, 1984, p. 6).

8. Of course, these fees did not accrue exclusively to the televised teams. The NCAA received a share, and each conference had its own revenue-sharing agreement.

For the next four-year television contract, the NCAA Television Committee dropped its exclusive arrangement with ABC and allowed ABC and CBS to telecast college football games for a total fee of $263.5 million (Falla 1981, p. 119). The Supreme Court voided this contract in 1984 when it upheld a lower-court decision that the NCAA television contract restricted output and fixed prices in violation of the Sherman Act (see section 7 below).

The NCAA's interest in output restrictions stretched beyond television appearances. Besides restricting the number of games that could be televised, the NCAA, through a certification process, also restricted the number of postseason bowl games. As many as fifty postseason games were played in the 1940s, but by 1952 only nine were played. The NCAA extended its restrictive policies in 1955 when the membership agreed to restrict the number of preseason practices and regular season games in football and basketball (Lawrence 1982, pp. 275–82). In subsequent years, the number of bowl games has risen and fallen; however, any new bowl game has to be certified by the NCAA.

Between 1950 and 1980, the popularity of college basketball blossomed. With the increased demand and revenues, the NCAA took a keener interest in regulating basketball's supply of games. For one thing, in order to take advantage of the increased demand, the NCAA expanded its basketball championship tournament at various times. In 1952 the tournament involved twenty-four teams; in 1953 it expanded to thirty-two; by 1979 it was up to forty-eight teams; and it presently involves sixty-four teams. One episode of special interest relating to restrictions on basketball occurred in 1960. Up to this point, the National Invitational Tournament (NIT) had been on a par with, and was sometimes superior to, the NCAA tournament. The NIT had a long tradition to it, and the small size of the NCAA field allowed the NIT a large pool of quality teams from which to choose. In 1960, the NCAA Executive Committee instructed members that conferences with automatic bids to the NCAA tournament should only compete in that tournament; also, any teams chosen "at large" (without automatic bids) owed their first allegiance to the NCAA tournament

(Falla 1981). From 1960 onward, especially with the onset of increased television exposure, the NCAA tournament began to dominate the NIT in prestige and money.

Each of these actions reinforces the idea that, despite the NCAA's public posturing, the association has functioned as a cartel. The reality of its actions reduced output, increased prices, and increased profits in intercollegiate athletics. Although some, including spokespeople for the NCAA, have suggested that the input restrictions merely maintain amateurism and competitive balance, the output restrictions are clear signs of rent-enhancing collusion. The only rationale, for example, behind the NCAA's study of television's impact on attendance is that of a profit-maximizing cartel. The monopolized television contract, the expansion of the basketball tournament, and similar actions fall squarely into the cartel explanation of NCAA behavior.

6. The NCAA's Control of Inputs, 1950–70

Along with the output restraints, between 1960 and 1980 the NCAA proliferated its rules pertaining to inputs in college athletics, especially with regard to athletes. The rules run the gambit from numbers of athletes and coaches to recruiting visits, allowable spending on recruits, and so on. Some of the more prominent restrictions which were instituted are described in what follows.

In terms of contact with recruits, many provisions were put in place over this period. The NCAA adopted provisions that allowed a school to contact an athlete only three times at off-campus locations and three times at the recruit's institution, with that institution's approval. A university was allowed to pay for one visit (coach class) by a prospective student athlete. The printed material a school can give to a prospective athlete is also strictly regulated along with the type of lodging, food, and entertainment allowable for recruits (*Manual of the NCAA* 1989–90, pp. 83–84).

Another restrictive provision agreed to by the NCAA was the National Letter of Intent. Basically, the National Letter of Intent binds a high school player to attend a particular university. After the National Letter of Intent is signed, no other school may attempt to recruit the student athlete. The letter also prohibits a student from enrolling in another school without losing two years of eligibility (Lawrence 1982, p. 382).

A cap has been placed on the number of scholarships that a school can award. Schools in Division I-A football are now limited to twenty-five new scholarships per year and an aggregate of ninety-five scholarships in a given year. Division I schools in basketball are allowed fifteen scholarships in a given year. Most other major sports also have ceilings on the number of scholarships that can be in effect per year (*Manual of the NCAA* 1989–90, pp. 148–50).

The list of input restrictions could go on to fill a volume by itself. In 1961, the NCAA adopted the five-year rule, which means that an athlete loses eligibility five years after first entering an institution. In 1965, a rule was passed to require athletes to maintain at least a 1.6 grade point average. The NCAA expanded enforcement powers and funding in the 1970s to complement these restrictions. After 1971, the NCAA Council served only as an appellate group; the Infractions Committee levied penalties against schools.

The NCAA has addressed problems concerning distribution of rents within the cartel. Early on, in 1958, it required participation in a minimum number of sports in order for a school to compete in any sport. At conventions held in 1974 and 1978, members agreed to divide the association into Divisions I (A and AA), II, and III. The reason for this division can be traced to what is known as the Robin Hood proposals. The Robin Hood proposals would have required that revenues accumulated from televised games and postseason bowl games be shared by all members of the NCAA in an egalitarian fashion. These proposals failed, but the "big time" universities were contemplating leaving the NCAA if they passed (Koch and Leonard 1978, p. 231). For Division I-A eligibility, a school has to schedule at least 60 percent of its contests against other I-A schools, have attendance at home games of at least seventeen thousand (a four-year average), have a seating capacity of thirty thousand, or be a member of a conference where at least six members sponsor football and at least one-half meet the above attendance requirements (*Manual of the NCAA* 1989–90, p. 274). Although some exemptions were granted, fifty universities were dropped from the ranks of Division I-A in 1982 (Koch 1983, p. 365).

All of the NCAA actions examined in this section are devices to lower a school's cost of producing output (athletic contests); that is, they are simple monopsonistic practices. The Letter of Intent can be construed as a signaling device to other schools that they need not spend resources on trying to persuade an already signed athlete to attend their university. Severe penalties were adopted for any athlete who attended a school other than the one for which he signed a Letter of Intent. By stipulating exactly how many times a school can visit a recruit and how much a school can spend in recruiting an individual athlete, and by spelling out what materials can be given to an athlete, the NCAA lowered the costs of recruiting by member universities. Granting freshmen eligibility can be seen as a cost-cutting device. Making freshmen eligible for football and basketball in 1972 allowed schools to use their athletes for four years instead of three, as was the case before freshman eligibility.[9] Most successful cartels are able to tailor rewards to relative contributions to cartel profitability, and the NCAA is no exception. The members of the NCAA in 1974 and 1978 agreed to adhere to a divisional alignment, enabling them to erect a barrier to entry into Division I athletic programs. As described above, restrictions were imposed on schools that wanted to enter Division I.

7. The Courts and the NCAA Television Plan

The single NCAA television plan had always met with some resistance. A major unsettling source was the restriction of appearances by popular teams. The restriction spread revenues around but, in doing so, took money away from some of the most successful programs. Even before its final downfall, the NCAA's single television plan had given ground. For instance, in 1978 the NCAA and ABC settled out of court with

9. The issue of freshman eligibility is not one-sided within the cartel. A 1989 NCAA basketball committee proposed abolishing freshman eligibility. Support for eliminating freshman eligibility most often emanates from more successful programs, which have a larger pool of talented players and, at times, an excess supply of such players. With no freshman eligibility, these schools would be able to alleviate their excess supply problem while leaving other schools with a shortage of talented players.

Warner Cable Communications, which wanted the right to televise Ohio State games on cable in Columbus (Falla 1981).

In the 1984 case of the *National Collegiate Athletic Association v. Board of Regents of the University of Oklahoma et al.*, the Supreme Court of the United States upheld lower-court decisions which stripped the NCAA of its monopoly power to negotiate the television contract for all universities. The University of Oklahoma and the University of Georgia argued that the individual members of the NCAA, not the NCAA itself, owned the property rights to televise college football. The schools argued that the NCAA Television Plan was a per se violation of Section 1 of the Sherman Antitrust Act through the actions of price fixing and the artificial restriction of output (Pacey 1985, p. 149; Porto 1985, p. 130). The NCAA argued that their Television Plan promoted the noncommercial undertakings of the organization, such as amateurism, keeping a competitive balance, stabilizing paid attendance at football events, and increasing cooperation among schools.

The courts found that the NCAA television plan restrained trade by preventing schools from selling athletic events at prices determined by the free market and by output levels. The arguments by the NCAA to justify its actions were found to be without merit, with the court concluding that NCAA actions were, in fact, cartelizing in nature. The federal district court in Oklahoma noted that the NCAA was a "classic cartel" that had

> almost absolute control over the supply of college football which is made available to the networks, to television advertisers, and ultimately to the viewing public. Like all other cartels, NCAA members have sought and achieved a price for their product which is, in most instances, artificially high. The NCAA imposes production limits on its members, and maintains mechanisms for punishing cartel members who seek to stray from these production quotas. The cartel has established a uniform price for the products of each of the member producers, with no regard for the differing quality of these products or the consumer demand for these various products. (*Board of Regents of*

the University of Oklahoma et al. v. the National Collegiate Athletic Association, 546 F. Supp. 1276 WD Okl. 1982, pp. 1300–1301)

With regard to the NCAA argument that a restricted television contract was needed to protect live attendance, the Supreme Court hypothesized that the NCAA's true motive resulted from "fear that the product (football games) will not prove sufficiently attractive to draw live attendance when faced with competition from televised games." The Supreme Court decision continued that, if the NCAA was correct and college football was a unique product and all television programs are substitutes, then "it would not be possible to protect attendance without banning all television during the hours at which intercollegiate football games are held."

Though the 1984 Supreme Court decision allowed schools to negotiate their own television contracts, breaking up some of the NCAA power over output, the NCAA still collects a 4 percent surcharge from the home team on all national telecasts. More important, the NCAA retains the power to keep a school off television through the disciplinary actions of the Committee on Infractions or the NCAA Council (*Manual of the NCAA 1989–90*, pp. 270, 313–14). Therefore, in spite of the NCAA's lack of the ability to control the negotiations of members' television contracts, it can use its enforcement powers to keep certain schools from obtaining lucrative television appearances. As noted earlier, in 1980 a nationally broadcast college game brought a fee of $600,000 and a regional telecast garnered $426,779, with up to 90 percent of that money going to a school (and its conference) if it competed in Division I.

8. Recent Developments

During the 1980s, a new wave of NCAA regulation has surfaced. This new wave has proceeded in terms of new restrictions as well as increased power for the enforcement of existing restrictions. Also, the legal process is redefining the framework in which the NCAA operates. In many cases this has strengthened the NCAA's position as a monopsonistic cartel. Finally, the internal structure of conference alignment is in a period of adjustment.

As in earlier years, the primary impetus behind the new restrictions came from two sources: (1) the increased demand for the NCAA's activities, and (2) widespread violations of NCAA rules. In its response to the increased demand and violations, the NCAA has passed new restrictions which have themselves been a source of controversy. Two significant restrictions are commonly referred to as Proposition 48 and Proposition 42. Both erect additional barriers to participation in college sports. Proposition 48 ties freshman eligibility to performance on the SAT/ACT college entrance examinations and a minimum grade point average in a core curriculum in high school. More specifically, a freshman student athlete is deemed a "qualifier" if he meets the following criteria: (1) he graduated from high school; (2) he completed a core curriculum of at least eleven academic courses; (3) he accumulated a grade point average of at least 2.0 in the core curriculum; and (4) he scored a combined 700 on the SAT math and verbal sections or a 15 composite score on the ACT. If a student athlete does not meet all of these requirements but does achieve a cumulative 2.0 grade point average in high school, he is deemed a "partial qualifier." A "nonqualifier" is a student athlete who meets neither the qualifier nor the partial qualifier criterion.

Under Proposition 48, a freshman qualifier is eligible for financial aid and may practice and compete for four years. A partial qualifier may receive institutional financial aid but may not practice or play for the school during his freshman year. More important, the partial qualifier loses one year of eligibility. Nonqualifiers are ineligible for financial aid, practice, or competition, and also lose one year of eligibility (*Manual of the NCAA* 1989–90, pp. 103, 110–11).

Proposition 42 revises and complements Proposition 48. It basically eliminates the category of the "partial qualifier." Therefore, it prohibits even those students who achieve a 2.0 cumulative grade point average from receiving institutional financial aid. Only those who meet the "qualifier" criteria of Proposition 48 are eligible for financial aid.

Both of these regulations have generated strong criticism from inside and outside the NCAA. The criticism largely centers around charges of racial bias. For instance, in men's basketball blacks account for well over 90 percent of the Proposition 48 casualties. While the provisions obviously impede black athletes proportionately more than whites, racial bias is not the most obvious or compelling motivation of the rules. Instead, both entry restrictions fit the cartel narrative. The restrictions transfer rents to some of the stronger and more academically developed schools and conferences. They are yet another means to limit competition for inputs. Blacks happen to suffer disproportionately from the regulations; yet this type of input restriction is in perfect harmony with past restrictions that have not attracted nearly as much attention.

Beyond the new NCAA regulations, the membership has adopted even more stringent penalties. Foremost is the so-called death penalty. Under this penalty the NCAA may suspend an athletic program found guilty of repeat violations within a five-year period. This penalty is not merely an idle threat as was a similar penalty under the Sanity Code. It has already been applied in the case of the Southern Methodist University (SMU) football program. The NCAA suspended SMU from competition for the 1987 and 1988 seasons, stripped the school of scholarships, and imposed limits on scholarships as the program attempts to rebuild. In addition to this new twist in enforcement, penalties in general have increased in severity. Oklahoma State University received a four-year probation for various recruiting violations. The sanctions included restrictions on scholarships, bowl appearances, and television appearances. Prior to this, the stiffest penalties usually covered a two-year probationary period.

The NCAA also emphasized cost control procedures in the 1980s. The association offers the services of specialists to member schools; these specialists review the expenditures and methods used by the various athletic programs. The emphasis on cost control and budgetary overspending comes at the same time that the demand for and the revenues from college sports continue to grow dramatically.[10] The NCAA basketball tournament alone netted revenues in excess of $70 million in 1988.

10. Projecting the image of operating losses helps the NCAA create an atmosphere on college campuses that encourages more input restrictions. Of course, a *budget overrun* for a particular part of a nonprofit institution is in no way analogous to an *economic loss* incurred by a for-profit firm. This point is discussed more fully in the next chapter.

The 1980s also witnessed an increase in legislative and judicial activity pertaining to the NCAA. In the *NCAA v. Tarkanian* (1988), the Supreme Court ruled that the NCAA, because it is a voluntary association, was not in violation of the due process provision of the Constitution. Tarkanian, the University of Nevada at Las Vegas head basketball coach, ran afoul of the NCAA during the 1970s and challenged the sanctions imposed on him. He questioned the legality of several standard procedures of NCAA enforcement including not giving the accused the chance to face his accusers or to review all the evidence. Some state legislatures and judicial bodies, in addition to forcing NCAA investigations in their states to adhere to due process, have enacted or are considering enacting increased penalties on sports' agents and alumni who make payments to players.

A very recent development is the interest by the U.S. Congress in the graduation rates of college athletes. Division I-A schools graduate football players at a slightly lower rate than that of the general student population. In the case of basketball, graduation rates fall substantially below that of the general student population. To this point, the congressional measures, if passed, would require schools to report graduation rates publicly.[11]

The NCAA stands to gain from many of these recent developments, especially some of the legislative actions. In essence, legislative restrictions on alumni and agents simply convert parts of the *Manual of the NCAA* into law. The laws dealing with alumni and agents allow the NCAA to police its cartel arrangement more effectively by bringing those outside the agreement under threat of legal penalties and by providing for enforcement resources from the public purse. Increases in penalties and the scope of enforcement enhance the profitability of collusion.

Another development of interest is also gathering steam. Throughout the century, teams have moved from one conference to another as their interests and financial realities have dictated. Still, in recent months some significant conference realignments have taken place or are being considered. In 1990

11. See *Washington Post*, September 13, 1989, section G.

several significant moves were made. Penn State joined the Big Ten; Florida State joined the Atlantic Coast Conference; South Carolina and Arkansas joined the Southeastern Conference; and Miami joined the Big East Conference. In addition to these changes, numerous other proposals for realignment have surfaced and are under active discussion. In the meantime, NCAA basketball conferences have been undergoing the same kinds of changes.

Why all of this newfound interest in realignment? Clearly, staying competitive in television markets and expanding those markets is a primary motive. During the 1980s, the Big East Conference illustrated the gains that could be made from tying several population centers together with respect to the value of a basketball television contract. To the extent that these shifts indicate competition among conferences, they may have the long-run impact of destabilizing the NCAA.

The most recent development of interest has been the decision on how to divide the revenues from the new $1 billion contract with CBS among the NCAA basketball tournament participants. Shares will be allocated by conference on the basis of the conference's performance over the past six years in the tournament, plus the scope of the conference member's overall athletic programs. A stated $25,000 per year per school will be allotted for academic enhancement. The NCAA has advanced this plan as a means to break the link between school performance and financial reward.[12] However, given that conference revenue-sharing agreements already existed, very little has changed. Revenues are dispersed on the basis of performance (measured per conference) and size of athletic programs. These have been two prominent factors in allocating rewards since the NCAA's inception and mute any redistribution from large to small schools.

9. Conclusion

The NCAA originally organized to solve an externality problem in college football, the problem of nonstandardized rules and violence during the course of play. Once individual schools began to meet regularly, the cost of additionally discussing

12. See *USA Today*, October 24 and October 25, 1990, section C.

input prices, recruiting practices, financial aid, and so on, was low. From the inception of the NCAA its members discussed methods of reducing their input costs by allowing only amateur athletes to compete in intercollegiate athletics and by restricting financial aid, but they had no enforcement mechanism to punish violators of these rules. In the early 1950s, NCAA members agreed to stricter recruitment and financial aid regulations and began enforcing these rules through the Committee on Infractions and the Council of the NCAA. Also in the early 1950s, the NCAA began to regulate the televised output of its members. The cartel, therefore, controlled both the input and the output markets of college sports and created an effective enforcement mechanism to punish violators of its rules.

Throughout the next thirty years, the NCAA continued to pass legislation to restrict output and lower the cost of inputs. In 1984, the Supreme Court ruled that NCAA control over output (television appearances) violated the antitrust laws. Despite this setback, the NCAA still has the power to deny a school appearances on television if the school has violated NCAA rules. As of this date, the NCAA continues to act as a classic cartel by coordinating the pricing of the input services of players and paying players less than the competitive market value for their services. It is this aspect of NCAA behavior, especially the enforcement of the cartel agreement with respect to players, that is the focus of the analysis that follows.

FOUR

Inside the NCAA

This chapter is descriptive in content. The discussion centers on the organizational structure, the stated goals and purposes, the finances, and the operational procedures of the NCAA. The basic idea is to introduce the reader to the complex inner workings of the NCAA, because several aspects of cartel behavior can be seen in the way the NCAA is organized and operated.

The chapter is organized as follows. Section 1 considers the NCAA from an organizational perspective. Who controls the NCAA? What is the scope of authority of different actors? Where does real authority lie? Section 2 surveys the financial workings of college athletics. Some estimates are offered of alumni giving, gate receipts, bowl game revenues, and other revenue sources, as well as of the costs of college athletics. Certain interpretative adjustments to these revenues and costs are necessary in order to gain an insight into the profitability of college athletics and to comment on the much discussed deficits crisis in present-day college athletic programs. Section 3 covers the rules governing NCAA members, coaches, and athletes and examines the most recent edition of the *Manual of the NCAA*, wherein are contained the explicit rules of this cartel with respect to student athletes. Some concluding remarks are offered in section 4.

1. An Organizational Overview of the NCAA

A few basic aspects of NCAA organization are widely known. The NCAA is a voluntary association of over one thousand educational institutions. Table 4 shows the growth in membership of the NCAA for selected years since 1906. The NCAA includes institutions of all sizes and academic quality. It has

TABLE 4
NCAA Membership, 1906–88

Year	Members	Year	Members
1906	38	1966	666
1907	49	1967	691
1909	69	1968	706
1912	97	1969	721
1924	135	1970	747
1945	216	1971	757
1949	317	1972	770
1950	387	1973	776
1951	415	1974	806
1952	430	1975	824
1953	456	1976	841
1954	477	1977	853
1955	489	1978	862
1956	506	1979	861
1957	539	1980	880
1958	549	1981	902
1959	567	1982	957
1960	582	1983	970
1961	597	1984	988
1962	614	1985	981
1963	623	1986	991
1964	645	1987	1002
1965	659	1988	1017

Source: *NCAA Annual Report* (Mission, KS: NCAA, 1989), pp. 27–28; and Jack Falla, *NCAA* (Mission, KS: NCAA, 1981).

four categories of membership: active membership, conference membership, affiliated membership, and corresponding membership. Each category has different requirements, voting rights, dues payments, and so forth.

Active members are those four-year accredited colleges which have been elected by a two-thirds vote by the NCAA Council and which follow the stipulated rules and obligations (they pay their dues, they maintain ethical and academic good standing, and so forth). Active member schools are eligible to compete in NCAA championships in their respective divisions and have a single vote on NCAA legislation. Current dues for active members are broken down as follows: Division I, $1,800 per year; Division II, $900 per year; and Division III, $900 per year.

A member conference is a group of schools which compete among themselves to determine a conference championship. The conference must have at least six members in a single division and compete in a minimum of four sports. A conference is elected to membership at the NCAA national convention or by a majority of the NCAA Council. Member conferences have the same voting privileges as active members. Their dues are as follows: Division I, $900 per year; Division II, $450 per year; and Division III, $450 per year.

Affiliated members are groups or associations concerned with at least one sport that is under NCAA jurisdiction. For example, the National Association of Basketball Coaches and the College Football Association are affiliated members. These members have no voting rights on NCAA legislation and their dues are $225 per year.

Corresponding members are those schools or organizations elected by the NCAA Council or Administrative Committee which are not eligible according to the previously mentioned membership criteria. They have no voting privileges and must pay dues of $225 per year (*Manual of the NCAA* 1989–90, pp. 7–16).

To handle this diverse membership, the NCAA divides itself into different divisions for athletic competition. In football the major programs compete in Division I-A. In 1988, almost one hundred schools competed at this level. Smaller programs compete in Division I-AA or Division II. Schools that do not grant scholarships compete in Division III.[1] In basketball, almost three hundred schools compete in the highest group, Division I. The smaller basketball programs are in Divisions II and III. Since 1950, the organization has added over six hundred new members. For all practical purposes, the NCAA today directs and controls all major revenue-producing collegiate athletic events.[2]

---

1. The nonscholarship status is somewhat misleading. While these schools do not offer scholarships solely on the basis of athletic ability, the financial aid process is influenced at many schools by athletic ability. In other words, two applicants, equal in academic ability but unequal in athletic ability (one an excellent quarterback and the other a nonathlete), are not equally likely to receive the same financial aid.

2. The National Association of Intercollegiate Athletics (NAIA) is another association of college athletic programs. However, the NAIA does not have a

The rapid expansion of the NCAA since 1950 reflects the inability of the cartel to control entry. For much of this period, entry was a means, particularly for the smaller schools, to share in the revenues of the larger and more successful schools. For the most part explicit revenue-sharing payments were (are) made within conferences. However, the smaller, non-revenue-producing schools were able to share in the large-contract television revenues by requiring a given number of lower-division games to be televised. The forcing of some schools into Division I-AA and the litigation over television rights in large part stemmed from this sharing with the smaller schools of the television revenues generated by the larger schools. Ultimately, the legal victory by the universities of Oklahoma and Georgia limited the degree to which the larger schools could suffer from the increasing NCAA rolls.

Undoubtedly, the NCAA's stated purposes recall the earlier days of the organization when the control of externality problems, such as the development of common rules, was paramount to the viability of the young organization. Obviously, the NCAA is not going to state explicitly that its central function is to control the wages of student athletes. Thus, the organization states that its purposes include the promotion of educational and athletic excellence; the setting up of eligibility rules related to scholarship, sportsmanship, and amateurism; the promulgation of rules of play; the collection of data; the supervision of play; the development of NCAA rules and regulations; and research on athletic competition (*Manual of the NCAA* 1989–90, p. 1). Most of these purposes sound innocent enough, echoing old rules from codes of amateurism and the Olympic Games. And some, such as establishing rules of play, are indeed an externality-controlling arrangement. Yet blended into this fabric of public-goods provision is a system of cartel rules with respect to the compensation of student athletes.

While the NCAA is a voluntary organization, it is not a loosely knit club that relies on self-restraint. Its organizational

---

network television contract and, in general, is an association of schools with small athletic programs. Many schools have switched affiliations from the NAIA to the NCAA. These are now Division I-AA, II, and III schools in the NCAA.

structure and mechanisms of control are well defined. Figure 1 presents an organizational chart of the major components of the NCAA. This is not a chart developed by the NCAA (see *Manual of the NCAA* 1989–90, p. 18); it is a construction based on our own analysis of the association and how it functions.

Obviously, the basis of the organization is its membership. The membership, however, does not maintain operational oversight or daily control of the association. Insofar as the

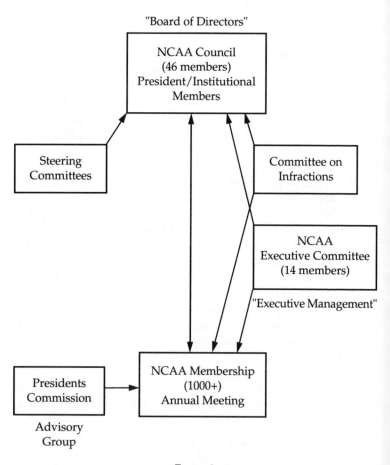

FIGURE 1
Organization of the NCAA

general membership meets annually at a convention (unless a special assembly is called), it functions much like shareholders in a corporation. Members vote (by majority rule) on general policies, officers, and committee assignments. As an appendage to the general membership, the Presidents' Commission studies and advises the association on selected issues and can request the convening of special sessions of the general membership. The Presidents' Commission was formed in 1984 and comprises the presidents (or their representatives) of forty-four NCAA institutions, twenty-two members from Division I and eleven members each from Divisions II and III.

At the top of the NCAA hierarchy, at least in terms of general policy control, is the NCAA Council. This group operates like a board of directors. It is made up of the NCAA president, secretary-treasurer, and forty-four institutional representatives. Specifically, the Council is empowered to set NCAA policy between conventions. More important, the Council interprets the constitution and bylaws, as set out in the *Manual of the NCAA*, between conventions and is the arbiter of last resort in issues concerning enforcement actions on member schools. Various steering committees, made up of Council members from the same divisional level, consider matters relating to their own divisions. However, a two-thirds vote of the entire Council can overturn a policy enacted by a steering committee.

The Executive Committee and the Committee on Infractions maintain actual managerial control of the NCAA. The Executive Committee, which consists of fourteen members, and its staff handle NCAA financial matters and oversee championships. The Infractions Committee investigates possible code violations and determines penalties. The executive officers of the NCAA are the Executive Committee members headed by the president. The Committee on Infractions has six members and is headed by the director for enforcement. It is the enforcement staff that does the bulk of the investigative work for the Infractions Committee. These groups operate out of NCAA headquarters in Overland, Kansas. Because of membership on both the Council and Executive Committee, the president wields more influence than any other single person in the NCAA. Over one hundred fifty staff are employed at NCAA headquarters.

Because of its prominent role, the Committee on Infractions warrants special attention. The committee does not perform the basic information-gathering function in an investigation. Instead, it initiates the investigative process. It may start the process because of allegations of misconduct by various sources (other schools, coaches) or because of evidence that strongly suggests misconduct. At the behest of the Infractions Committee, the enforcement or investigative staff of the NCAA searches for evidence and takes depositions from key figures. If the investigative process at the preliminary level turns up questionable practices, a more detailed investigation follows. The institution under investigation is then notified by the enforcement staff of its possible violation of NCAA rules. After the investigation the Infractions Committee reviews the evidence, questions the relevant institutional representatives and/or players, and issues its findings and any sanctions. At this point the institution may make an appeal of the finding and/or sanctions to the NCAA Council.

One aspect of NCAA organization which will be critical in the later analysis is that the enforcement staff in Kansas is not nearly large enough to survey and monitor the practices of the over one thousand schools that make up the NCAA membership (indeed, it's not large enough to monitor even one hundred of the large programs). The enforcement officials act upon information given to them by people in the field, such as coaches and competitor schools. Enforcement of the cartel rules in the NCAA takes place outside cartel headquarters in the competitive process during which schools compete for student athletes. This is a key point to keep in mind. It means that NCAA investigators will rely on indirect and probabilistic evidence to guide initial decisions as to which schools to investigate.

Finally, a word is in order about the income statement and balance sheet of the NCAA as an organization. Most of its revenues come from conducting championships. In fiscal year 1989, for example, of the $98.2 million collected in revenues by the NCAA, over 75 percent came from the Division I men's basketball championship and 7.9 percent came from other championships. Membership dues accounted for $870,000 (*NCAA News*, June 20, 1990, p. 14). After dispersals to member schools, the NCAA headquarters retained control of over $22 million. This comes to about $146,000 "worth of control" per NCAA employee.[3] The NCAA is a plush organization, and there is ample evidence of typical nonprofit behavior where employees have been treated quite generously in terms of perquisites. A case in point is the use of NCAA funds as the source of no-interest loans to NCAA executives.[4] Another example, very common in nonprofit settings, is the recent completion of a new, multimillion dollar headquarters facility for NCAA executives.

2. NCAA Finances

This section offers some perspective on the "profitability" of college athletics. The NCAA's rhetoric would lead one to believe that the vast majority of schools are operating in the red.[5] Recent books by Telander (1989) and Sperber (1990) reinforce this view by attacking the "myth" that most college athletic programs make money. While there are difficulties in arriving at a precise "bottom line," it is possible to establish some bounds in terms of the financial success of college athletics.

There are a couple of stumbling blocks to such an analysis that should be noted at the outset. Much of the self-reported NCAA data on revenues and costs are aggregated across institutions without reporting institutional-level data. Also, revenues are not reliably reported for many important areas. For instance, payments to coaches for endorsements, television programs, shoe contracts, and the like are not included as athletic revenue for the institution, although they may provide more than half of a coach's compensation. A further problem is that precise figures for alumni contributions are not available. Most athletic foundations through which such funds flow are

3. This is based on a staff size of 150.
4. See *Washington Post*, November 19, 1985.
5. See Sperber (1990), who argues that most schools are in the red. Skousen and Condie (1988), two accountants at Utah State University, discuss many of these problems and estimate revenues and costs for the Utah State athletic program on the basis of standard accounting procedures rather than university budgetary procedures. They found that, although the program was in a budgetary deficit, true revenues exceeded true costs attributable to athletics. Boreland, et al. (1989) pursued a similar study at Western Kentucky University. These studies are discussed below.

not legally part of the university so that public access to such data is limited. Moreover, the cost data supplied by institutions, even without the nonprofit incentive problem discussed above, usually exceed the costs important for economic decision making. At many schools, excess capacity exists in classes, dormitories, and food production so that the marginal cost of providing these services to athletes is very low. Yet most institutions cost these services close to the dollar value paid by an average student. In a similar vein, the revenue generated from athletic events is often allocated to some other budgetary unit in the university. This causes reported budgetary revenues to understate the true revenues attributable to athletics.

For these and other reasons mentioned below, accurate financial data on the NCAA and its members are hard to uncover. In what follows, some estimates of relevant figures are presented. The word "estimate" should be emphasized; the numbers at best enable an order of magnitude insight into the finances of college athletics.

Published and Estimated Revenues and Expenses

Table 5 presents the trends in revenues for 192 Class A (Division I-A or I-AA football) schools, as well as total revenues for all schools in 1985 as reported by the NCAA. The mean revenue for Class A schools increased from $2.4 million in 1977 to $4.8 million in 1985. The table breaks down revenues attributable to football and basketball for a few years between 1973 and 1985. Aggregate revenue for all NCAA schools for 1985 is reported as $1.064 billion.

Because the definition of Class A includes Division I-AA schools, the mean revenue figures understate the average revenue for the major, Division I-A schools. Table 6 gives a better picture of the latter institutions. It presents the frequency distribution of schools with $5 million in revenue or more. In total, fifty-seven Class A schools had revenues of over $5 million in 1985. Even more instructive, twenty-five schools exceeded $9.0 million in revenues. These figures are understated in that they do not include much of the compensation received by coaches.

Obviously, a large portion of total institutional revenue comes from gate receipts. Estimation of gate receipts is difficult. Most

TABLE 5

Aggregate Revenues as Reported by the NCAA
for Class A Schools

Year	Mean Revenue (in millions)	Mean Football Revenue (in millions)	Mean Basketball Revenue (in millions)	Total Revenue* (in millions)
1973	—	$1.0	$.15	
1977	—	1.3	.27	
1978	$2.4	—	—	
1979	2.6	—	—	
1980	3.0	—	—	
1981	3.4	1.9	.45	
1982	3.5	—	—	
1983	4.2	—	—	
1984	4.6	—	—	
1985	4.8	2.5	.71	$1,064

Note: Class A schools are schools which played Division I-A or I-AA football in 1985.
Source: Mitchell H. Raiborn, *Revenues and Expenses of Intercollegiate Atheletic Programs* (Mission, KS: NCAA, 1986).
*Total for all schools (classes A–F). Class A = $921 million.

TABLE 6

Frequency Distribution of Athletic Revenues
for Major Schools in 1985

More than (in millions)	Less than (in millions)	Number of Schools
$5.0	$6.0	8
6.0	7.0	8
7.0	8.0	12
8.0	9.0	4
9.0		$\underline{25}$
		$\sum = \overline{57}$

Source: See table 2.

schools have a variety of ticket prices without providing information on how many tickets are sold at a given price. Ticket allocation based on price discrimination schemes prevails at many institutions, where contributions to the schools' athletic programs govern the allocation of choice tickets that may have

TABLE 7

1989 Football Attendance and Estimated Gate Receipts

School	Total Attendance (6 games unless otherwise stated)	Gate Receipts (in millions)
Michigan	632,136	$8.85
Tennessee	563,502	7.89
Ohio State	511,812	7.17
Penn State	501,870	7.03
Auburn	577,556 (7 games)	8.09
Georgia	489,210	6.85
Clemson	472,902	6.62
Nebraska	534,086 (7 games)	7.48
Alabama	438,258	6.14
Michigan State	433,896	6.07
Florida	573,144 (8 games)	8.02
LSU	425,334	5.95
South Carolina	492,429 (7 games)	6.89
Oklahoma	414,156	5.80
Washington	406,350	5.69

	Attend.	Gate Receipts
Total attendance for Division I-A, 1989	25,185,784	$352.6
Division I-AA, 1989	4,731,664	66.2
Division I-A + I-AA, 1989	29,917,448	$418.84

Sources: Total attendance is from *NCAA News*, January 3, 1990, p. 16. Gate receipts are estimated by multiplying total attendance by an average ticket price ($14).

the same face value as other tickets. In addition, some teams share receipts or charge different prices for games at special sites. The procedure here was to take 1989 attendance figures for the fifteen Division I-A schools with the highest average attendance and multiply them by an "average" ticket price.[6] Table 7 presents these data. The perennial attendance and revenue leaders are Michigan and Tennessee. In 1989, Michigan garnered almost $9 million and Tennessee almost $8 million from estimated gate receipts. The schools listed are estimated

6. These "average" ticket prices were obtained from either the programs handed out at football games or the ticket offices of the various schools. A common price was $14, which by 1990 was closer to $17.

to have received $105 million in 1989, or, on average, approximately $6.97 million per school. In fact, for this same year the top fifty-five schools drew at least two hundred thousand spectators, which roughly translates into at least $3 million in gate receipts per school.

Television rights are also a large revenue source for the NCAA and its members. As discussed in chapter 3, initially the NCAA bargained with the television networks and granted an exclusive contract to a particular network for coverage of regular season games. By the early 1980s, the networks were competing for coverage rights, and the NCAA began allocating games to more than one network. The 1984 Supreme Court decision broke up the NCAA's ability to negotiate a single contract. After this date several conferences formed the College Football Association (CFA) and negotiated their own television contract. The Pacific 10 and Big Ten conferences joined to sign a separate television agreement. In all of these arrangements, the schools appearing on the telecasts receive payments which are subject to the conference's revenue-sharing agreement. Table 8 presents 1983 revenues by conference. For 1983, the Southeastern Conference topped all others by a wide margin, with over $11 million in television revenues; with ten schools in the conference, each member received an average of $1.1 million. The per-school average for the conferences listed ranges

TABLE 8
1983 Network Television Football Revenues by Conference
(in millions)

Conference	Revenues	Revenues/Member
Southeastern	$11.2	$1.12
Pacific 10	7.5	0.75
Big Ten	7.1	0.71
Southwest	6.8	0.75
Big Eight	5.8	0.72
Atlantic Coast	4.6	0.58
Western Athletic	2.8	0.31
Northern independents	8.3	—
Southern independents	4.2	—

Source: See table 7.

TABLE 9

Estimated Network Television Revenues by School, 1984
(in millions)

School	Revenues	School	Revenues
Oklahoma	$3.2	Notre Dame	1.8
Florida	2.2	Nebraska	1.6
Georgia	2.0	Ohio State	1.5
USC	2.0	Michigan	1.5
Texas	2.9	Iowa	1.5
Auburn	1.9		

Note: The revenues are subject to conference revenue-sharing agreements, except in the case of Notre Dame, which is not affiliated with a conference. Source: Computed from information given about scheduled appearances and payments per appearance for national, regional, and cable telecasts in the *1984 NCAA Television Committee Report.*

from $0.31 million for the Western Athletic Conference up to the Southeastern Conference figure of $1.1 million. Table 9 presents estimates of television revenues generated by institutions in 1984. Oklahoma's estimate tops the $3 million mark. Very recently, Notre Dame broke ranks with the CFA and signed its own $36 million contract with NBC. The television contract for the NCAA basketball tournament now rivals and even exceeds the football contracts. CBS recently signed a multiyear package for the NCAA basketball tournament worth over $1 billion.

Alumni giving is another significant revenue source, but one that is difficult to estimate empirically.[7] The alumni-giving

7. Some estimates for major schools were compiled by the *Boston Globe* and the *Omaha World Leader,* and are reported in Hart-Nibring and Cottingham (1986) and Coughlin and Erekson (1984). These sources discuss some of the problems of obtaining accurate estimates for such items as in-kind gifts (services, oil, cattle) and special fund-raisers for facilities, equipment, and so on. The estimates themselves suggest why relying on survey data for alumni gifts is problematic. For some schools and conferences, the figures are quite believable. For example (in the *Boston Globe* figures), North Carolina heads the Atlantic Coast Conference with $5 million in gifts and Duke is last with $1 million. In contrast, though, some figures are inconsistent with reasonable expectations. Michigan, one of the larger revenue-producers, is listed at $600,000, which is about the level of giving at Western Kentucky University. Oklahoma is listed at $2,024,000, and Texas is listed at $600,000. These figures may not be incorrect insofar as the budgetary procedures at these schools are

TABLE 10

Estimated Alumni Contributions to Athletics, 1986
(in millions)

School	Alumni Giving	School	Alumni Giving
Texas A&M	$4.9	Southern Methodist	2.2
Florida	4.5	Mississippi State	2.2
Iowa	2.6	Auburn*	1.7
LSU	2.5	Texas Tech	1.1

Source: Computed by summing minimum of gift category sizes and number of givers in each category as listed in the programs given out by these schools at football games.

*Donations for football only. In other cases, it was not always clear from the source whether the contributions included all athletic contributions or only football. Also, some schools have other clubs and foundations which provide support for athletics.

clubs, as listed in many programs of college sporting events, were employed to obtain the average contribution to such clubs. These average contributions were summed to obtain estimates of alumni contributions. Typically, these programs list donors and give a range for the level of giving (in some cases phone calls were made to obtain the range). For instance, at the University of Florida the "Bull Gators" category contains donors of $10,000 or more per year. In 1986, this group listed ninety-six contributors. If the estimates contain a bias, it is downward. Sums were obtained by using the minimum giving level in each category. Also, some givers chose to remain anonymous. Most problematic are the "endowed" gifts, which provide a continuing income source. These were estimated at the level of a full scholarship. Table 10 presents these data for several Southeastern, Big Ten, and Southwest Conference schools. These estimates, though, provide only a small sample of alumni gifts because some of the biggest revenue generators

concerned, or they may be net after "expenses"; yet they almost certainly understate the value of athletic contributions to these schools. One common practice is for these revenues to be held and spent in entirely separate accounts by athletic staffs. Thus, at the end of the year the net transfer to the university appears to be zero if all money in these accounts is spent. However, a net increase in capital assets (scoreboards, facilities, and so on) often results so that the net impact on the university is not zero but positive.

in this area, such as Michigan, Ohio State, and Alabama, do not provide enough information about their athletic foundation on which to base estimates.

So far, the focus has been on football revenue. However, college basketball revenue has grown at a faster rate. Table 11 presents data on total basketball revenue from the NCAA Division I tournament for 1989, as well as per-conference allotments for the 1989 tournament. The 1989 championship had gross receipts of over $70 million. Of this amount, $34.1 million was disbursed to schools in the tournament. Participants in each round received $274,845 each. Doing the simple addition, $549,689 went to those in the second round, $824,534 went to regional semifinalists, and $1.1 million went to those who reached regional championships. An additional $1.00 million went to teams for Final Four participation. Each school that went to the Final Four grossed $2.1 million. As table 11 shows, the distributions to conferences and their institutions was led by the Atlantic Coast Conference and the Big Ten, whose conference and members earned almost $5 million, followed by the Big East with $4.1 million, and the Big Eight and Pacific 10 with approximately $2 million each (*NCAA News*, July 19, 1989, p. 1).

The preceding year, 1988, is the last year for which detailed receipts and expenses for the men's basketball championship are available. Gross receipts were $68.2 million, of which $57.8 million came from television rights and $9.1 million came from ticket sales. The cost of putting on the tournament was $12.5 million. This included a $6.8 million grant to the National Collegiate Foundation. This left net receipts of $55.7 million, of which $29.7 went to competing schools and $3.5 million went to conferences. Amazingly, $22.65 million went to the NCAA itself, an increase from the $17.46 million received in 1987. Thus, the NCAA got 40 percent of *net* receipts (after expenses) in 1988 and the same percentage in 1987 (*NCAA Annual Report 1987–88*, pp. 67–68). It should be noted that the NCAA ran a surplus seven of the eight years following 1980, the largest surplus being in 1987–88 in the amount of $13.3 million. The average surplus for the years 1980 through 1988 was $4.5 million per year (*NCAA News*, January 4, 1989, p. 1).

Several other sources contribute to college athletic revenues. Football bowl game receipts have grown to large proportions.

TABLE 11

1989 National Collegiate Division I Men's Basketball
Championship: Analysis of Distribution of Net Receipts

Conference or Institution	Total Members	Total Tournament Games	Distribution
Atlantic Coast	8	18	$ 4,947,205
Big Ten	10	18	4,947,205
Big East	9	15	4,122,672
Big Eight	8	8	2,198,758
Pacific 10	10	7	1,923,913
Metro	7	6	1,649,069
Southeastern	10	5	1,374,225
Big West	10	4	1,099,379
Southwest	9	4	1,099,378
Western Athletic	9	4	1,099,378
Atlantic 10	10	3	824,534
Midwestern	7	3	824,534
West Coast	8	2	549,690
American South	6	2	549,689
DePaul	1	2	549,689
ECAC No. Atlantic	10	2	549,689
Mid-American	9	2	549,689
Notre Dame	1	2	549,689
Ohio Valley	7	2	549,689
Sun Belt	8	2	549,689
Big Sky	9	1	274,845
Colonial	8	1	274,845
East Coast	8	1	274,845
Ivy League	8	1	274,845
Metro Atlantic	8	1	274,845
Mid-Continent	8	1	274,845
Mid-Eastern	9	1	274,845
Missouri Valley	8	1	274,845
Northeast	9	1	274,845
Southern	8	1	274,845
Southland	8	1	274,845
Southwestern	8	1	274,845
Trans America	10	1	274,845
Totals	266	124	$34,080,748

Source: *NCAA News,* July 19, 1989, p. 1. (Does not include additional disbursement for Final Four.)

Table 12 lists the growth of bowl receipts per team from 1968–69 to 1988–89. Teams today receive from $500,000 to more than $6 million for a bowl appearance. These revenues increased significantly in the latter 1980s with the emergence of corporate sponsorship of many of the bowls. The 1989 Rose Bowl (even without a sponsor) contributed a total of almost $15 million to the revenues of USC, Michigan, and their respective conferences.

Information on costs relevant for economic decision making is difficult to obtain, especially at the institutional level. Most of the data come from the official NCAA report on finances, which reports only aggregates, means, and percentages. However, from this source and others a few revealing facts about costs can be deduced.

Table 13 reports two items of interest. First, the average athletic expenditures for Class A institutions from 1973 to 1985 are given. These data suggest drastic increases in costs of over 180

TABLE 12
Growth in Bowl Receipts per Team
from 1968–69 through 1988–89

Bowl	1968–69	1973–74	1978–79	1983–84	1988–89
All American	No game	No game	$154,312	$450,000	$800,000
Eagle Aloha	No game	No game	No game	No game	500,000
Mobil Cotton	$340,150	$475,092	1,527,606	1,884,362	2,500,000
Florida Citrus	NA	80,033	127,509	500,000	1,000,000
Freedom	No game	No game	No game	No game	550,000
Hall of Fame	No game	No game	No game	No game	1,000,000
Independence	No game	No game	60,910	400,000	500,000
John Hancock Sun	75,000	102,408	200,000	402,000	750,000
Liberty	151,215	222,865	342,684	574,311	1,000,000
Mazda Gator	210,000	243,014	387,750	679,444	1,000,000
Orange	335,000	997,000	1,128,077	1,839,540	2,800,000
Peach	NA	NA	172,781	418,888	900,000
Rose	925,000	1,420,000	2,116,834	5,608,877	6,150,000
Sea World Holiday	No game	No game	218,645	412,000	850,000
Sunkist Fiesta	No game	184,934	342,562	817,831	2,500,000
USF&G Sugar	240,000	450,206	975,109	1,800,000	2,750,000

Source: *Sports Inc.*, November 21, 1988, p. 32.

TABLE 13

Athletic Expenses, 1973–84, and Percentage Breakdown
for 1985 for Class A Schools

Average Expenses		Breakdown for 1985	
Year	Expense	Type	% of Total
1973	$1.64*	Salaries and wages	30%
1977	2.21	Grants-in-aid	17
1981	3.24	Team and other travel	12
1985	4.60	Guarantees and options	8
		Equipment and supplies	5
		All other	28

Source: See table 2.
*In millions.

percent at a representative institution. However, beyond the
obvious inflation adjustment, it should be emphasized again
that "expenses" reported by nonprofit institutions are not the
"costs" of economic analysis. The incentive structure in the
NCAA and at individual schools does not encourage schools to
report as large a "profit" or surplus as possible. The second
part of Table 13, a percentage breakdown of operating expenses for 1985, is instructive on the possible skewing of expenses. Salaries and wages head the list at 30 percent. This
includes the salaries and wages of coaches, athletic directors,
and athletic staff personnel. Grants-in-aid total 17 percent of all
expenses. The average "cost" of a full scholarship was computed by the NCAA report to be $5,930. Of course, this figure
ignores the presence of excess capacity and other fixed costs,
and therefore the marginal costs of adding athletes at many
schools may be lower. Travel expenses (for players and recruiting) plus equipment and supply expenses for all sports total
only 17 percent of all expenses. The "all other" category of
expenses is not explained in the report. If grant-in-aid expenditures are adjusted even slightly for the excess capacity and
fixed cost situations across schools, the total of the three primary areas of player-related expenses (tuition, room and
board, travel and equipment) is about the same as or less than
administrative and coaching salary expenses. Contrast this situation to that of a professional sports team. The Boston Celtics

are traded as a partnership on the New York Stock Exchange so that public data are available on their operations. Player-related expenses and player salaries account for over 50 percent of the Celtics' total costs.[8]

Moreover, these data do not tell the whole story. While coaches' salaries are hard-dollar costs for institutions, coaches of large programs are subsidized from outside the university setting. In effect, this represents another revenue source for institutions, although the monies usually pass directly to the coach. Table 14 shows the estimated official salary and outside compensation for several football and basketball coaches and athletic directors in 1986. The point is not a normative one of whether such salaries should or should not be paid. Obviously, coaches must be kept on their relevant supply curves. The point is the proper assessment of institutional revenues.

As can be seen from the tables presented here, revenues are large at the major NCAA schools. The typical big-time program's revenues exceeded $9 million per year by NCAA accounts. By adding up revenues from the various tables and including basketball gate and regular season television receipts, this figure is more likely in the $13–$20 million range.

Of course, according to the NCAA's figures, costs are about equal to or exceed revenues, even at the major institutions. A case in point is the University of Michigan. Table 15 presents the revenues and expenses as reported by that school's athletic department. In spite of revenues in excess of $18 million, the school reported a loss of over $2 million. Taken at face value, this would appear to confirm the tenuous financial position of college athletics. However, alumni gifts to Michigan's "M-Club" do not appear to be included among the revenues and, as discussed below, other problems exist with using these self-reported, unadjusted figures.

Adjustments to Revenues and Costs

The apparent equality of revenues and expenses of some schools in the NCAA's study, the large number of programs experiencing budget deficits, and the apparent losses incurred by a program such as the University of Michigan's all point to

8. See Standard and Poor's *Stock Reports* and company surveys.

TABLE 14
Annual Compensation of Football and Basketball Coaches
and Athletic Directors as of 1986

Coach	Base Pay	In-Kind and Outside Compensation
		Football
Jackie Sherrill (Texas A&M)	$114,190	$130,000 for media shows and endorsements; $200,000 insurance policy; up to $150,000 for house; two cars
Bo Schembechler (Michigan)	108,102	10 football season tickets; dealer-provided car; camp facilities; TV show privately negotiated
Joe Paterno (Penn State)	100,000 +	TV show; use of car; media advertising
Ray Perkins (Alabama)	120,000	$10,000 + from media show; $10,000 + for consulting services; $60,000 for shoe contract
Pat Dye (Auburn)	90,000	Deed to home after 20 years (by alumni); $25,000 shoe contract; $10,000 + from media shows; $10,000 + consulting; $10,000 + retail companies
		Basketball
Jim Valvano (North Carolina State)	85,000	Shoe contract = $100,000; TV-radio shows; 3 cars provided; endorsements; 40–50 speeches at $5,000 each
Dean Smith (North Carolina)	100,000	Shoe contract = $100,000; bonus for NCAA Tournament; camp
Bob Knight (Indiana)	89,000	Shoe contract = $100,000; TV-radio shows; car; camp; tickets
Eddie Sutton (Kentucky)	79,000	Shoe contract = $125,000; camp = $10,000 in 1985; bonus for NCAA tournament; tickets
John Thompson (Georgetown)	N.A.	Shoe contract = $165,000
Jerry Tarkanian (Nevada–Las Vegas)	155,393	10% of revenue from NCAA tournament; shoe contract; camp; TV-radio shows; car; 234 tickets
		Athletic Directors
Frank Broyles (Arkansas)	71,531	10 football tickets a game; bonus for bowl appearances; open-ended contract
Dick Schultz (Virginia)	94,000	Use of car; 35-seat football box/30-seat basketball box
Doug Dickey (Tennessee)	74,000	$10,000 expense account; $10,000 annuity; use of car; country club membership; 6 football and 4 basketball tickets

Sources: *USA Today*, section C, September 24, 1986. Basketball: *USA Today*, December 4, 1986, and *Sports Illustrated*, November 16, 1988.

TABLE 15

University of Michigan Reported Athletic Finances, 1989
(in millions)

Revenues		Costs	
Football receipts	$7.4	Salaries	$5.6
Basketball receipts	1.8	Recruiting, travel, equip.	4.6
Hockey receipts	.2	Grants-in-aid	3.6
Championships, bowls	2.4	Facility maintenance	3.0
Royalty fees, camps	2.6	Administrative costs	2.6
TV and radio	1.9	Debt service	1.7
Concessions and souvenirs	1.5		
Athletic facility fees	.7		
Totals	18.5		21.1

Source: *U.S. News and World Report,* January 8, 1990, p. 52.

a single apparent conclusion. College athletics is, on average, no more than a break-even proposition and is often a money loser, even for large schools. The financial situation of college athletics thus appears to be in dire straits at the present, and the NCAA has expressed its concerns in this regard.

One might ask if college sports lose money or, at best, break even, why do colleges put more and more dollars into facilities, salaries, and the like? In one respect a traditional financial analysis of college athletics ignores the fact that colleges and universities are not-for-profit entities that are governed by accounting procedures that tend to aggregate the revenues and costs of given units of these organizations, such as the economics department, the music program, the business school, the liberal arts college, or the athletic program. When disaggregated properly, the financial conditions of college athletic programs may not be so dire. To see how this might work, consider the following issues.

The first veil over college sports revenue and cost data is the organizational structure. Colleges and universities are organized on a nonprofit basis. Because of this, no one has a claim on revenues left over after costs. Executive officers do not have a fiduciary responsibility to maximize the difference between revenues and costs. Because revenue surpluses cannot be taken home by college executives or returned to shareholders, they are captured by preferences for expenses on the job. As in most nonprofit settings, reported costs tend to rise to equal or exceed revenues. This fact by itself helps to explain the apparent equality of average revenues and expenses in the NCAA's own study.

Many of the expenses incurred by universities and their athletic programs, once their nonprofit status is taken into account, are more accurately described as indications of surpluses rather than costs. Some expenses would not occur or would be far less without the need to find some expense area into which to slot anticipated revenues; that is, these "costs" exceed those which would occur if the executive had to maximize surpluses for shareholders. Examples of such expenses are operating expenditures on non-revenue-producing sports and capital budget expenditures. For instance, the new $12 million "Hall of Champions" at the University of Michigan is a classic case of huge surpluses finding their way into a large expense category. Another example would be the new, state-of-the-art athletic offices for basketball coaches at the University of Kentucky. Some expenditures on athletic personnel and salaries could also be included in this category of allocating anticipated surpluses.

Accounting practices at universities also make it difficult to interpret NCAA and institutional data. (1) Institutions often do not match revenues and costs with the budgetary unit responsible for generating or incurring them. (2) Institutions often lump irrelevant fixed costs onto athletic budgets. These practices have the net result of increasing athletic department costs and decreasing revenues.

Universities, like any type of firm, must pay "hard" dollars to outside suppliers of goods and services. However, within the university and between budgetary units, prices and the flow of dollars are often artificial and fictitious. Revenues generated by one unit are attributed to some other unit or to the general revenue fund. Costs may also be distributed in arbitrary ways among units. The point is not to criticize such practices. As with other nonprofit firms, these practices serve some functional purpose. However, the use of revenue and cost data for drawing conclusions about the well-being of any one unit can be misleading without certain adjustments.

In the case of athletic departments, it is not unusual for food concession revenues and souvenir vendor revenues (or at least some portion of them) to be allocated to some other university unit, such as food services or the general fund. The value of such revenues and contracts at big-time programs is not trivial, running into the millions of dollars. Revenues from other game day sales such as parking, additional bookstore purchases, and increased cafeteria use may also not be included in the athletic department's budget. Likewise, revenues from any increased enrollment or general giving from alumni or others due to athletic success may be difficult to estimate and are simply lumped into general revenue categories. Yet even small impacts (in percentage terms) on enrollment can lead to large increases in revenues. For example, if a school with twenty thousand students attracts two hundred (or 1 percent) of those as a result of athletics (or its advertising) and each student pays $2,000 per year in tuition, the school gains $400,000 from tuition alone.

Beyond the arbitrary allocation of revenues in university accounts, university accounting systems rarely, if ever, attempt to measure the true additional costs incurred by athletics, that is, the dollars which would *actually* be saved if athletics were dropped. For instance, a large expenditure category for athletic programs is grants-in-aid for tuition, room, board, and books. Most often, these grants to athletes are "priced" at their retail value in the athletic budget rather than at their true cost to the university. For example, actual food costs are usually only about 40 percent of their retail value. The athletic department pays the general fund the retail value, which overstates the actual cost to the university by 60 percent. The end result is that the general university fund (or some unit) receives an implicit subsidy. If the university dropped athletics, only the actual food costs would be saved. The same principle holds for tuition grants-in-aid as long as the school is below full capacity. If an athlete's registering does not displace other students from registering, the university does not lose tuition. In addition, to teach two hundred to three hundred athletes does not require many, if any, additional faculty. Taking these points into account in some cases cuts the grant-in-aid costs by over half.

Taking these two points together would radically change the "bottom line" estimates for most college athletic programs. Two accountants, Skousen and Condie (1988), undertook to reexamine the finances of Utah State University's athletic program. According to the school's published finances, the program lost about $800,000 per year. But Skousen and Condie found that, once revenues and costs were allocated correctly and irrelevant "costs" excluded, the program actually returned over $300,000 per year. (This does not take into account any enrollment impacts.) A similar study at Western Kentucky University by Boreland, Goff, and Pulsinelli (1989) showed that a supposed $1.5 million loss was actually a loss of no more than $300,000 and actually turned into a surplus if estimates of enrollment impacts were taken into account.

Applying these principles to the large revenue producers would in almost every case yield large surpluses where schools supposedly are suffering losses from athletics. Looking back at the self-reported revenues and costs for Michigan in table 15 highlights what we have been saying. First, as noted, booster giving does not appear to be allocated to the athletic department revenues. At Michigan, the value of gifts related to athletics, whether through athletic channels or not, must run into the millions. Second, while concession (including souvenir) revenues are listed as $1.5 million, this figure almost certainly understates the full value of these revenues, whether direct or from contract vendors. Considering only football attendance (one hundred thousand per game times six home games), this would imply that the university ultimately receives only $2.50 per fan in concession revenues. With basketball attendance included, the per-fan revenues would fall to just over $2.00. Third, the $3.6 million the school reported spending on grants-in-aid overstates the actual costs of adding athletes to classes, and purchasing their food and books for the reasons discussed above. With three hundred athletes, the reported figure would imply the average grant-in-aid per student to be $12,000. The actual cost *to the university* of adding three hundred more students to classes and purchasing food and providing housing for them is probably closer to 10 percent of this figure. Fourth, the general tendency for surpluses to find their way into expenses can be seen in the Michigan data. To some extent, salaries, facilities maintenance, administrative costs, and debt service all reflect expense preferences which would not exist if the program operated on a for-profit basis.

Colleges and universities have several reasons for converting their surpluses into expense preferences. For one thing, athletic programs constantly prod boosters for gifts. The difficulty of this job would increase if the university reported a large athletic surplus. Also, disguising surpluses allows university executives to transfer funds around the campus at their discretion, without stirring debates among departmental units. Disguising surpluses also reduces the pressure to compensate college athletes at higher rates. The rationale is that, if the school is losing money, how can it afford to pay athletes? Finally, as discussed above, the nonprofit nature of college athletics means that surpluses will find their way into expense categories.

Distribution of Surpluses

It is no secret that the NCAA as a cartel generates large amounts of total rents. Where do the rents flow? Most of them go to institutions in the NCAA, to the NCAA itself, and to the fraternity of head coaches. Players, of course, fare better than room, board, and scholarship when they receive secret payments, and such payments would mute the redistribution to coaches and institutions that the NCAA rules mandate. But a good guess is that such payments are not sufficiently high to alter the fundamental flow of rents to the cartel directors. Cheating may be widespread, but even in the most publicized violations the amount of secret payments is trivial in comparison to school and coaching revenues. Also, as one would expect, the most vociferous defenders of NCAA policy tend to come from the ranks of school executives and coaches.

The return of some of the surpluses to the NCAA executive staff and headquarters is evidenced by two events in particular. NCAA staffers took no-interest loans from NCAA monies in order to purchase personal items. Such a practice is not likely to occur within an organization on its last financial legs. What is more, the NCAA recently completed construction of its new headquarters in Overland Park, Kansas, another example of an "expense" which is more accurately an allocation of surpluses.

The flowing of surpluses to institutions is seen in some of the cases already mentioned. Large capital budget projects such as the Hall of Champions at the University of Michigan represent the expenditure of surpluses by an institution. Other athletic expenditures, whether for facilities for non-revenue-producing sports or for plush training facilities for football, also demonstrate the flow of rents. Implicit transfers to the general fund by means of the accounting practices discussed earlier also represent the allocation of surpluses.

Coaches are among the key recipients of surpluses. The data presented in table 14 on coaching salaries and benefits provide a glimpse of this redistribution. Additionally, the staffs, graduate assistants, volunteer coaches, and managers, at least in part, reflect returns flowing toward coaches and athletic directors. The data we have presented suggest that, while the NCAA talks of cost control and sometimes even takes steps to limit coaching personnel and some other expenses, cost containment does not extend to head coaches, athletic directors, and capital projects.

A few points should be made concerning the distribution of rents between coaches and schools. First, as in any nonprofit organization, control over rents will translate into things other than higher salaries. Head coaches, for instance, will increase their real income by hiring more or better assistants to ease the work of coaching and recruiting. Athletic directors will build more elaborate office facilities and will gain in reputation by promoting nonrevenue sports. After these in-kind benefits are included, what determines the relative share of cartel rents to coaches and schools? A question might arise as to why schools do not capture all of the rents, given the sometimes fierce competition for coaching positions. However, even with such competition, some coaches are better than others, and this is reflected in the value of their reputational capital. This type of capital is portable and allows these coaches to garner some of the available rents. Second, although coaches do compete for positions, the pool of all potential head coaches possesses some monopoly power. This derives from the fact that the cooperation of coaches is crucial to the stability of the cartel. Coaches possess knowledge of the cartel and of the facilitating institutional and alumni practices. Should coaches be paid only a competitive wage, they would become less likely to advocate cartel stability and more likely to oppose the redistribution of rents from players. Institutions, on the other hand, maintain certain assets which allow them to share in the cartel rents, namely, fixed capital assets such as stadiums, training facilities, and brand names.

While coaches and athletic departments reap many of the fruits of athletic success, universities are not necessarily at the mercy of their athletic departments. As noted earlier, the NCAA membership and Council are not made up solely of coaches and athletic directors. University executives and faculty are also NCAA members and functionaries. In 1990, of the twenty-two Division I members on the Council, nine were nonathletic executives or faculty, including two university presidents and one vice-president. Also, regardless of the separation which may exist between some universities and their athletic departments as accounting units, university presidents and regents possess ultimate hiring and firing authority over athletic personnel. A few coaches may gain reputations which allow them a good deal of personal discretion; yet, as the case of former Ohio State football coach Woody Hayes and the infamous punching incident shows, even coaching legends can come crashing down. What we are getting at here is that, despite the disclaimers of university executives, college athletic programs by and large function under the direction of university executives and regents rather than in opposition to them.

The Value of Athletes to Schools

How valuable are athletes in terms of revenue to their schools? Ideally, to answer this question one would estimate a production function for team wins based on performance and then estimate the marginal impact of a win upon revenues. Due to the lack of reliable revenue data across a large number of schools, such an estimation procedure is not feasible. Thus, a somewhat more descriptive and piecemeal approach must be adopted. In general, however, the issue is, What is the contribution of players to winning games, and how does winning alter school revenues?

Some sources have already asked these questions with respect to individual players. Patrick Ewing's contribution, for instance, can be broadly estimated. Before he arrived at Georgetown University, the school had never reached the NCAA Final Four. After he left, it has not reached it again. While he played, Georgetown reached the championship game three times. Each Final Four appearance was worth close to $1 million. The tournament victories each year leading up to the Final Four spot amounted to another $1 million. Additionally, Georgetown played on national television numerous times during Ewing's tenure there. In total, Ewing accounted for about $12 million in increased revenues for Georgetown. This does not even take into account the stream of revenue Georgetown has accumulated since his departure that is a result of his fame. Similar procedures have produced figures running into several million dollars for stars like Bo Jackson at Auburn (where the school added an entirely new football seating section) and Doug Flutie at Boston College. The story would be the same for other elite athletes.

These figures give some idea of the marginal value of star athletes, but what about the typical player? The NCAA basketball tournament provides some insights on this issue. The marginal revenue value of a victory in the tournament is approximately $300,000 for a win and about $1 million for a win leading to the Final Four. Let us assume that the marginal contribution to a win of all of the players together is 50 percent. (This number seems appropriate since professional basketball players account for about 50 percent of team expenses and are, on average, not likely to be compensated above their marginal value products.) Let us also assume that a typical starter's marginal contribution to a victory is one-fifth, or 20 percent, of all players' marginal contributions. Given these assumptions, the typical player's marginal contribution to revenues from a tournament victory would be $300,000 times 0.50 times 0.20 = $30,000. If the team advanced to the fourth round, the player's contribution would be $120,000. If the team reached the Final Four, the contribution would be $120,000 plus $1 million times 0.50 times 0.20 = $220,000. Again, this would represent the marginal contribution of the typical player to tournament revenues alone. Total season contribution to revenues would have to include the player's impact on gate receipts, television appearances, and alumni gifts.

Such a hypothetical case only crudely substitutes for a systematic estimation of player marginal revenue products. Yet it provides some insight into the order of magnitude of player MRPs. The implicit compensation of tuition, room, and board (about $5,000 to $10,000 per year at most schools) is undoubtedly only a fraction of the typical player's revenue contribution.

3. The NCAA Manual: A Reader's Guide to the Cartel Rules

A comprehensive review of NCAA rules is not possible because the rule book is almost four hundred pages long and is newly issued each year. Instead, the most recent *Manual of the NCAA* (hereafter *NCAA Manual*) is reviewed to highlight some specific mechanisms of cartel operation. Three areas are the focus for discussion: recruiting, eligibility, and enforcement. The purpose is to show the degree of detail and thought that has gone into the running of college athletics. Sometimes, the vision of the administration of athletics is one of haphazard actions by individuals with more ability to teach blocking techniques than to manage a large industry organized as a buyers' cartel. A sample of the rule book suggests that the control of the NCAA cartel is not accidental or haphazard. In contrast, the rules cover the most minute details of the relationship between schools and athletes and present over four hundred case studies. The *Manual* is much more akin to a legal, statutory code than to a loose collection of club rules.

Recruiting

The explicit recruiting bylaws of the *Manual* cover a range of situations. Operating Bylaws Article 13.01.3 states, "A member of an institution's athletics staff or a representative of its athletics interests shall not recruit a prospect except as permitted by this Association." This article continues to cover "legal" contact with prospective athletes, publicity of potential recruits, personnel who may scout, tryouts, transportation for visitation, number of contacts with a recruit, and behavior at sports camps and clinics. A representative of the university's athletic interests, as defined by the NCAA (*NCAA Manual* 1989–90, p. 71), is an individual who is known (or *should* have been known) by members at the institution to have promoted or financially contributed to athletics at the university, or has been asked to recruit or assist a prospective student athlete. "Once an individual is identified as such a representative, the person retains that identity *indefinitely*" (*NCAA Manual* 1989–90, p. 71, emphasis added). Any such person is prohibited from offering aid to the prospective student athlete even if such aid is offered to prospective students in general. Among the actions that are specifically prohibited are the arrangement of employment of relatives, gifts of clothing or equipment, the cosigning of loans, the provision of loans to friends or relatives, gifts of cash or any merchandise, and the granting of free or reduced-rate housing (*NCAA Manual* 1989–90, p. 82). The *Manual* pays special attention to expense-paid visits to campuses. An institution may finance only one visit to campus for a student athlete. The rules surrounding such a visit are quite detailed with respect to transportation, entertainment, transportation for parents or others (not allowed), and even the quality of the meals the student athlete may enjoy during a visit.

The basic idea of the recruiting rules is to hold down the dissipation of cartel rents. Without such constraints on recruiting competition, schools would vigorously go after superior athletes and in the process transfer cartel rents to players and their families rather than to coaches and institutions. In fact, some of the anecdotes regarding recruiting suggest that a good deal of rent seeking does occur in recruiting in spite of the rules. In any event, the NCAA recruiting rules are a rational cartel attempt to control costly rent-seeking behavior by member schools.

Eligibility

The *Manual* details the eligibility regulations for players. The most basic rule states that "the student-athlete shall complete his or her seasons of participation within five calendar years from the beginning of the semester or quarter in which the student-athlete is first registered." (*NCAA Manual* 1989–90, p. 106). Exceptions are permitted for student athletes who enter the armed services, who go on official church missions, or who are involved in U.S. government foreign aid service. This provision places a so-called five-year clock on an athlete that applies across all sports. Two years of football followed by four years of baseball is not permissible. Actual participation can only occur during four years with special exceptions for injury or illness (*NCAA Manual* 1989–90, p. 109). Also, athletes must satisfactorily complete at least twelve semester hours of academic work during any enrolled term (*NCAA Manual* 1989–90, p. 116). This applies whether the athlete is on scholarship or not. In essence, an athlete may not be a part-time student who works and takes "football" as a class as another student might take "chorus" as a part-time study.

In the section on freshman eligibility, a controversial provision concerning SAT scores has been included in the bylaws. Operating Bylaws Article 14.3.1 states that, to be eligible for institutional financial aid and to practice and participate in intercollegiate athletics (to be a "qualifier"), a freshman must complete a core curriculum in high school with at least a 2.0 grade point average and must score at least a combined 700 on the SAT or a 15 on the ACT. A freshman who does not achieve the minimum GPA or SAT/ACT but does achieve a cumulative 2.0 grade point average can receive aid but is unable to practice or play his first year. Also, he loses one year of eligibility. This is known as Proposition 48. Successful matriculation of twelve or more hours per semester does not regain the lost year no matter what grade point average is achieved. Proposition 42, which went into effect in August 1990, revises Proposition 48 for Division I freshman athletes. It eliminates the category of "partial qualifier" (cumulative grade point average of 2.0); thus, only qualifiers can get financial aid, can play, can practice, and have four years of eligibility.

The eligibility rules are often an expression of intra-NCAA power struggles. This is the case with the issue of freshman eligibility based upon SAT/ACT scores and minimum grade scores. Certain schools within the NCAA stand to gain an advantage on the playing field and hence at the box office from such rules. We analyze this case in detail in chapter 6.

Enforcement

The rules regarding enforcement are also detailed in the *Manual*. The General Principles to this section sets out a broad mandate for NCAA enforcers. It states that administrators and coaches "must do more than avoid improper conduct or questionable acts." Further, "The enforcement policies and procedures are an essential part of the intercollegiate athletics program of each member institution and require full and complete disclosure by all institutional representatives of any relevant information requested by the NCAA enforcement staff, Committee on Infractions or Council during the course of an inquiry" (*NCAA Manual* 1989–90, p. 265). In practice, this gives the Committee on Infractions the power to punish schools by asserting noncooperation in addition to the power to punish schools by proving wrongdoing. The burden of proof is placed upon the accused in any NCAA inquiry.[9]

The enforcement provisions empower the Committee on Infractions to consider complaints against member institutions, to revise policies and procedures, to determine facts related to allegations (through use of the investigative staff), and to impose penalties (*NCAA Manual* 1989–90, pp. 265–71). This makes the Committee on Infractions the policing agency, the prosecuting agent, and the arbiter regarding the misconduct of members. The Committee on Infractions or the executive director channels complaints to the investigative staff. The staff can then conduct a preliminary investigation or a complete one. After the information is gathered, the Committee on Infractions may issue a censure or reprimand if it views the violation as secondary or nonserious. If the allegation is major, an official letter of inquiry is sent to the member school regarding the charges. The member is expected to gather all the relevant information at its disposal. Allegations have a four-year statute of limitations unless the Committee on Infractions deems a willful pattern of misconduct to be present.

At this stage the *Manual* calls for a hearing at which the concerned parties appear before the Committee on Infractions.

9. University of Nevada, Las Vegas, basketball coach Jerry Tarkanian is a case in point. Accused and convicted by the NCAA of wrongdoing, Tarkanian sued the NCAA to avoid the probation that had been imposed on him. He charged that the NCAA violated his right of due process. Ultimately, after district and appellate court victories, Tarkanian lost a 5–4 decision in the Supreme Court. However, the high court did not hold that Tarkanian had been granted due process; instead, it rejected the applicability of the due process argument because of the voluntary nature of the NCAA.

At the hearing the investigative staff presents its information. The member institution then presents its explanation. The committee can exclude oral or written material it deems irrelevant or repetitive. Committee members may question persons appearing before it. These persons may be represented by one personal legal counsel. The committee then meets privately and determines liability and penalties under the broad provision to use information "it determines to be credible, persuasive and of a kind which reasonably prudent persons rely on in the conduct of serious affairs" (*NCAA Manual* 1989–90, p. 363). A majority vote decides whether the findings of the committee are accurate. For a major violation there is a minimum penalty that must be applied.

One interesting aspect of the process is the degree of secrecy involved. No recordings, electronic or stenographic, may be made by member institutions or persons questioned at hearings. Only handwritten notes may be taken. The committee tape-records the hearing, and institutional representatives may listen to but may not make verbatim records from the tape (*NCAA Manual* 1989–90, pp. 355–66).

What is apparent is that one can hardly be given a "fair trial" with these procedures. This means that it is not in the interests of the NCAA to provide such institutional arrangements conducive to the fair treatment of members. In a cartel even allegations of cheating are dangerous to the stability and future of the organization. Once on the docket, even though the alleged cheater may be "innocent," a cartel will generally discipline a firm for even the appearance of impropriety.

4. Concluding Remarks

Studying the nuts and bolts of the organization and rules of the NCAA could fill a volume in itself. In this chapter some aspects of the NCAA's organization, finances, and rules have been highlighted. In the overall scope of this book, this chapter points out some of the descriptive characteristics and statistics concerning a well-functioning cartel. Economists are sometimes accused of passing over the details of the real world in favor of developing technical theories and using econometric techniques. While this criticism may have some foundation, the point of this chapter is to emphasize that the organization and behavior of the NCAA at a descriptive level are consistent with our characterization of the NCAA as a cartel. The NCAA is a voluntary association and hierarchy, yet one that is precluded in most other U.S. industries by the antitrust laws. NCAA revenues are growing rapidly, and school expenses are being skewed toward those who gain from the input cartel arrangement. Finally, in the NCAA rules, one sees both the detail of control and the broad enforcement powers that help to keep member institutions from engaging in profitable violation of cartel rules while others live by the standards.

FIVE

NCAA Enforcement

The preceding chapters provide a theoretical, historical, and descriptive discussion of the NCAA as a cartel. In this chapter some of the testable implications of viewing the NCAA as a cartel are pursued. In particular, this chapter focuses on the NCAA enforcement process. Though most economists accept the idea that the NCAA functions as a monopsony, explicit analyses of the enforcement process have been lacking. That is, which schools are investigated and put on probation and why?

The theoretical model of enforcement presented in chapter 2 guides the empirical study in this chapter. The model stresses the indirect and probabilistic ways in which cheating on the cartel is detected. Direct and constant surveillance of member schools and their associates is prohibitively costly for the NCAA. To avoid such costs, the NCAA investigative and enforcement staff will use easily observable variables, such as variability in winning percentage, to guide its enforcement decisions. It will also rely upon reports by competitor schools as a basis for determining whether an enforcement action is justified. To put it plainly, when a team has not won the conference championship in several years and suddenly improves its record and wins, the school becomes a suspect for recruiting violations and eventual NCAA probation. Evidence of this behavior is presented in this chapter. Also considered is the redistribution that is a by-product of such an enforcement strategy (the protection of perennial athletic powers, which have large brand-name and physical asset advantages in the marketplace for college athletics).

This empirical study of the enforcement process proceeds as follows. Section 1 discusses the theoretical model and the institutional setting of enforcement in more detail. A few of the points already covered in the earlier chapters which are important for the discussion of enforcement are briefly reviewed. Section 2 develops and tests a logit model of NCAA enforcement actions. Data from almost eighty schools over a thirty-year period are pooled to form a large cross-section study. In addition to the logit analysis, the experiences of "convicted" schools over time are examined. For example, do enforcement actions significantly alter win-and-loss records of the "convicted" teams during their postprobation periods, and do offenders become repeat targets of enforcement? Section 3 offers some concluding remarks.

1. NCAA Enforcement: Theory and Practice

The basic problem in any cartel is the incentive that exists for individual firms to cheat on the agreement. The NCAA is no exception in this regard; individual coaches, alumni, and schools stand to benefit from violating the NCAA agreement while other schools adhere to it. Winning coaches are wealthier coaches. Higher winning percentages are a signal of higher-quality coaching and raise the coach's opportunity wage in the market for coaches. Winning schools are wealthier schools. The most successful football teams are the ones drawing more fans to the stadium and generating additional revenues from regular season television appearances and from invitations to postseason bowl games. A school may receive increased financial support from public and private sources as a result of increased exposure from a nationally ranked football program. The quality of students who apply for admission to winning schools may improve (McCormick and Tinsley 1987). Alumni are happier when their alma mater wins on the gridiron. These rewards provide incentives for coaches, schools, and alumni to offer recruits wages above those set by the cartel as a whole. Any one school can gain an advantage over its competitors by attracting higher-quality athletes with the offer of wages above those paid by other cartel members. In deciding whether or not to engage in such behavior, the agents involved in recruiting athletes will balance the expected gains from violating the agreement against the sanctions imposed if they are caught times the probability of detection.

In order to make the sanctions a viable threat to potential violators and to reduce the profitability of cheating, a cartel must be able to detect violators. The NCAA Committee on Infractions polices the recruitment process and tries to detect illegal activities and to enforce the monopsonistic wage rules. However, the enforcement staff of the NCAA is small compared with the size of the cartel it polices. In 1988, the enforcement and compliance services staff consisted of twenty-eight employees; there are over one thousand institutions in the NCAA (*NCAA Annual Report* 1987–88, p. 21). Thus, member institutions must play the basic role in the detection of cartel violations; they must monitor each other for signs of illegal activity.[1] The Committee on Infractions then investigates the allegations brought before it, assesses the extent of violations, and levies penalties.

One method that individual cartel members can use to discourage cheating is to monitor the activities of other schools directly. Direct monitoring reduces the ability of schools to offer illegal inducements to recruits and players without detection. Such evidence may exist in the form of canceled checks, cosigned loans, travel accounts, letters, and so on, but this evidence is difficult and costly to find. Complete direct monitoring of a rival's recruiting practices would require constant surveillance of its coaches and alumni as they attempt to recruit potential players. Because this is prohibitively costly, schools will seek more efficient methods to monitor rivals' recruiting behavior.

More generally, as Stigler (1964) discusses, cartels will use probabilistic or indirect evidence to spot firms that are violating the cartel agreement. In the case of secret price cutting, no direct evidence will exist about cheating, so cartel members will resort to the use of probabilistic evidence. Similarly, NCAA cartel members will use probabilistic or indirect evidence as a guide to the amount of cheating being done by their rivals. In a word, NCAA members and the Committee on Infractions will monitor outputs rather than inputs (Alchian and Demsetz 1972).

---

1. The attorney for Mississippi State University, Erwin Wards, made this point during the 1978 congressional hearings.

Perhaps the best indirect evidence of illegal payments to players is a team's competitive performance. Certain aspects of a team's performance offer probabilistic evidence of violations. For example, the variability of a team's won-loss record provides indirect evidence of their compensation practices. A perennial break-even team that begins consistently to attract higher-quality athletes and to produce a winning record will cause rivals to infer illegal practices (higher wage rates). The rivals will initiate an investigation by the Committee on Infractions (or the committee itself may choose to investigate) of whether violations are being committed.

A related method of cartel enforcement resides in the recruitment process. Suppose two schools are bidding for an athlete. The loser knows that it was outbid, and thus it can turn in its rival to the NCAA. Greater success in recruiting can thus lead to increased scrutiny by the cartel. This method of cartel enforcement is closely related to the output monitoring hypothesis for a simple reason: there is a link between recruiting and winning. Success in the recruiting wars will reveal itself on the playing field. It seems clear, therefore, that winning variance proxies recruiting variance.

Returning to the winning variance argument for a moment, note that, for the hypothesis to hold strictly, upward and downward movements in winning percentage must lead to an increased propensity to enforcement and probation. It would seem that the theory only admits of an improvement hypothesis; that is, teams start to improve by making illegal payments that, if detected, would ultimately lead to probation. Nevertheless, the hypothesis can also be consistent with a decline in winning percentage. The enforcement process may be sufficiently slow as to lead, for example, to public revelations of violations prior to sanctions and probation. In the interim a team may halt the illegal payments as a way of showing "good-faith" efforts to correct the violations and start to lose more games as the quality of its inputs declines.[2] On this interpre-

2. In 1985, for instance, Texas Christian University unilaterally disclosed evidence that some of its athletes had received illegal payments and dismissed these players in mid-season. The team's record during its remaining games was dismal. At the end of the season, the school was placed on probation by the NCAA.

tation, variance of winning percentage is the appropriate predictor of cartel enforcement activities.

This enforcement process leads to redistribution within the cartel in the sense that NCAA enforcement will concentrate on schools that are consistent winners. The NCAA redistributes wealth by punishing up and coming teams that recruit players away from traditional winners. If this is the case, consistently higher winning percentages will not by themselves bring about higher probabilities of enforcement action. Thus, the NCAA functions, at least in effect, as an agent for major college athletic programs with long histories of fielding winning teams.

2. Empirical Tests

A Logit Analysis of Enforcement Actions

As an initial test of the hypothesis of output monitoring among NCAA members, a testable model of NCAA enforcement is presented. First, the general ceteris paribus conditions that, along with winning variability, are expected to influence the probability of enforcement are identified. The following general model presents these factors:

$$\text{prob[ENFORCEMENT]} = f \text{ (winning variability; other probabilistic variables; direct monitoring costs; amount of cheating).}$$

The role of winning variability has already been discussed; however, this may not be the only indirect, probabilistic means from which to infer cheating. Also, the costs of direct monitoring in a given situation will influence the likelihood of enforcement. For a given amount of cheating by a school, lower direct monitoring costs make the job of detection for member schools and the NCAA staff easier. An enforcement action is more likely, given some amount of cheating, as detection costs fall. Finally, the more a school cheats (or, as a first approximation, the demand for cheating), the more likely that cheating will be detected. Our winning variability model of enforcement does not imply that all schools cheat to the same extent. Certainly, some schools' alumni, coaches, and fans have a relatively more voracious appetite for winning and fewer scruples about cheating to gain such an end.

The following model is posited as a testable expression of this general enforcement model (all data are for 1953–83 unless otherwise specified):

$$\text{ENFORCEMENT} = b_0 + b_1 \text{ CV} + b_2 \text{ CV}^2 + b_3 \text{ DC} + b_4 \text{ SCPOP} + b_5 \text{ AGE} + b_6 \text{ STAD},\qquad(1)$$

where

ENFORCEMENT	= 1 if a school's football program has been put on probation and 0 otherwise;
CV	= the coefficient of variation of a school's football winning percentage;
CV^2	= the coefficient of variation squared;
DC	= the interaction of DCONF and CCHAM, where DCONF equals 1 if a team has switched conferences and 0 otherwise, and where CCHAM is equal to the number of conference championships won by the school (before or after a switch);
SCPOP	= the average number of secondary schools in the state of each institution in 1960, 1970, and 1980, divided by the population of the state in the same years;
AGE	= the founding date of each school; and
STAD	= the size of a school's football stadium, averaged over 1960, 1970, and 1980.

The dependent variable ENFORCEMENT designates whether a school's football program was placed on probation over the 1953–83 period.[3] Table 16 lists the eighty-five schools

3. The basic data source is U.S. House of Representatives (1978). We supplemented these data for the 1978–83 period with information from various United Press International (UPI) polls identifying teams which have been placed on NCAA probation (see *Washington Post* 1978–83, various issues). For

Table 16
NCAA Football Enforcement Actions, 1953–83

No Probation	No Probation	Probation
Air Force	North Carolina State	Arizona
Alabama	Northwestern	Arizona State
Arkansas	Notre Dame	Auburn
Army	Ohio State	California
Baylor	Oregon State	Clemson
Boston College	Penn State	Colorado
Brigham Young	Pittsburgh	Houston
Cincinnati	Purdue	Illinois
Colorado State	Rice	Kansas
Duke	Rutgers	Kansas State
East Carolina	Stanford	Kentucky
Florida	Syracuse	Miami (FL)
Florida State	Temple	Michigan State
Georgia	Tennessee	Minnesota
Georgia Tech	Texas	Mississippi State
Indiana	Texas–El Paso	Oklahoma
Iowa	Texas Christian	Oklahoma State
Iowa State	Texas Tech	Oregon
Louisiana State	Tulane	South Carolina
Louisville	UCLA	Southern California
Maryland	Utah	Southern Methodist
Memphis State	Utah State	Southern Mississippi
Michigan	Vanderbilt	Texas A&M
Mississippi	Virginia	Tulsa
Missouri	Virginia Tech	Wyoming
Navy	Wake Forest	
Nebraska	Washington	
New Mexico	Washington State	
New Mexico State	West Vriginia	
North Carolina	Wisconsin	

Sources: U.S. House of Representatives, "NCAA Enforcement Program," Hearings before the Subcommittee on Oversight and Investigations of the Committee on Interstate and Foreign Commerce, 96th Congress (1978, pp. 1480–1520), and *Washington Post* (1978–83, various issues).

---

the 1953–78 period, teams were defined as violators if their football programs were placed on probation and if the probation included television sanctions. For 1978–83, the violators were those schools identified by the UPI poll.

in our sample, classifying them in terms of whether or not they have had major sanctions levied against them.[4]

The difficulty of the authors of the present volume in finding data on enforcement is suggestive in itself. Like any cartel, the NCAA maintains secrecy with regard to its enforcement strategy. This is evidenced by what happened during the 1978 U.S. House of Representative hearings. The subcommittee chairman, John Moss, and Walter Byers, then executive director of the NCAA, engaged in a heated correspondence over the disclosure of documents. Representative Moss, when opening the hearings, commented on the difficulty encountered by congressional staff members in getting documents when he said "People are afraid of being perceived or perhaps misperceived as cooperating with this subcommittee." He accused Byers of feeding documents at his own pace and of organizing noncompliance among schools and opposition by other congressmen. The authors of the present volume attempted to obtain a list of enforcement actions from the NCAA. Although this information is widely publicized at the time of imposition of sanctions, the NCAA refused our request.

CV measures the variability of each school's winning percentage. (The mean winning percentages, standard deviations, and coefficients of variation for each school are listed in appendix 1 of this volume.) CV is a measure of output variability which provides indirect information about a school's compensation practices. Cartel theory suggests that a higher variability of winning percentage will raise the probability of investigation and probation. For example, take two rival teams, Western U. and Eastern U. If Western U. has a very low winning percentage for several years and then suddenly has a championship team, it is likely that Eastern U. will alert the Committee on Infractions to possible violations. Teams that compete for players will turn in teams with upwardly mobile winning records. As discussed earlier, the enforcement process may hit the violator as its

4. The data set was restricted to schools which play in major conferences and to major independent schools, that is, to cases where cartel monitoring and potential cheating on the cartel represent a real problem. Beginning with the membership of what is now known as Division I-A, we determined the final sample size by eliminating those schools for which observations on one or more of the independent variables were missing.

winning record is rising, or with a lag after it has ceased player payments and started to lose. In any event it is the variance of winning percentage that drives enforcement. The square of the coefficient of variation, CV^2, controls for a diminishing effect of winning variability on enforcement actions.

DC is another variable that is an indirect indicator of cheating. It controls for teams that have switched conferences and have also won conference championships. Both of these events serve as an additional signal that a school is a potential violator. On the one hand, if a switcher previously competed successfully either in some other conference or as an independent football power, its new conference opponents will suspect that the earlier winning records were related to rule violations. This will be especially so if the switcher rapidly achieves success at the expense of its new rivals (the University of Arizona and Arizona State University in the Pacific 10 Conference and the University of Houston in the Southwest Conference are examples of teams that were put on probation soon after changing conferences or becoming conference members). On the other hand, a champion that withdraws from a conference, especially after having been penalized, will be suspected of carrying its illegal behavior to the new competitive venue. In both cases the combination of mobility and success raises the probability that the NCAA's "competitive balance" is being disturbed. DC is therefore expected to have a positive sign—an increase in DC will lead to a higher probability of probation, all else equal.

SCPOP proxies the cost to cartel members of directly monitoring competition for inputs. An obvious way for schools to achieve a higher winning percentage is to recruit the best players from secondary schools. In a state with more secondary schools the difficulty of directly monitoring recruitment practices across universities is increased. Because of this increased monitoring cost, schools in those states will violate the rules more often, other things the same. The coefficient on SCPOP will have a positive sign because more cheating will lead to a higher probability of detection.[5]

5. Schools obviously recruit across state borders, blurring the effect captured by this variable. It is nonetheless useful to try in some fashion to control for the costs of directly monitoring rivals, and this is the best proxy that could be devised.

The variable STAD proxies the demand for football under the assumption that stadium sizes have adjusted to the demand for seats. A common problem in cartels is that individual members often have different demand-cost configurations. In the NCAA a school that faces a relatively higher and more inelastic demand for its football program has more incentive to pay athletes an above-the-cartel wage. The higher and the more inelastic the demand for its football program, the more likely a school is to engage in cheating because the gains are higher. More cheating leads to a higher probability of detection, ceteris paribus; therefore, STAD will have a positive sign.

The AGE variable is a proxy for the number of alumni of a school. AGE is also an indicator of the demand for football and a proxy for the amount of cheating taking place. An older school has more alumni and more football tradition. As the pool of alumni and their loyalty becomes greater, the demand for better football performance increases and becomes more inelastic. One way for a college to increase its chances of establishing or maintaining a winning football program is for a supporter to give payments and other perquisites (jobs, cars) to recruits and players. Older schools will be prosecuted more, other things equal.

Equation (1) is estimated by means of a logit analysis. This technique constrains the predicted values for the binary dependent variable, ENFORCEMENT, to fall between 0 and 1.[6] The results are reported in table 17. All of the explanatory variables are significant at the .05 level for a two-tailed test.[7] Although the coefficient of multiple determination is biased downward in this type of analysis relative to a model with a continuous dependent variable, the logit estimation of equation (1) accounts for 33 percent of the variation in enforcement actions across schools. This percentage is quite high given the aggregated and pooled nature of the underlying data.

---

6. The LOGIT procedure of SPSS[x] was used, which transforms the log odds ratio to produce values similar to those derived from the probit model. The response function is given by $\ln p/(1 - p)2 + 5$. See SPSS[x] User's Guide (1986, p. 605).

7. Equation (1) was also estimated with a probit model. The results are nearly identical to those reported in table 17.

TABLE 17

LOGIT Analysis of NCAA Enforcement Actions

Variable	Coefficients/(t-statistics)
Constant	−25.60964
	(−2.461)*
CV	29.08742
	(2.267)*
CV^2	−33.37897
	(−2.273)*
DC	0.52742
	(2.145)*
SCPOP	0.20829
	(3.023)**
STAD	0.01161
	(2.288)*
AGE	0.00002
	(2.417)*
R^2	.325
N	85

Sources: Data on NCAA sanctions are from U.S. House of Representatives, Subcommittee Hearings, "NCAA Enforcement Program" (1978, pp. 1480–1520), and from the *Washington Post* (1978–83, various issues). Data on wins and losses, conference switching, conference championships, and stadium sizes are from *College Football U.S.A., 1869–1971* (1972, pp. 502–8) and from the *World Almanac* (1960, 1970, 1980). Data on the number of secondary schools are from *Digest of Education Statistics* (1962, various pages). Data on the founding date of schools are from *Universities and Colleges* (1982, various pages).
*Significant at .05 level for a two-tailed test.
**Significant at .01 level for a two-tailed test.

The coefficient of variation CV has a positive and significant sign. Higher variability in a team's winning percentage leads to a greater probability of the NCAA taking action against that school. This result supports the output monitoring hypothesis. The interaction term, DC, is positive and significant. Winning teams that switch conferences face a higher probability of sanction by the NCAA. This result suggests that rival teams use conference switching and quality performance as a signal of illegal activity. The dispersion of secondary schools, SCPOP, also has a positive and significant influence on NCAA sanctions. If there are few high schools, college teams and their agents can monitor each other's recruiting activities directly, at less cost, and thereby can discourage cheating. If there are many high schools, the costs of monitoring college recruiting increase, and the likelihood of cheating and sanctions increases. The proxies for demand for a school's football output, STAD and AGE, are both positive and significant. Other things equal, schools with a higher demand for successful football programs are penalized more than schools with a lower demand for football programs.

Independent schools are not members of conferences. Notre Dame, for example, is an independent school that recruits nationally rather than regionally. This makes it more costly for regional schools to monitor Notre Dame's recruiting behavior in other parts of the country. Moreover, conference schools have less of an incentive to monitor independents because they do not compete directly against them in conference play. Thus, independents may be less likely to be convicted of violations. We estimated the logit model in equation (1), including a dummy variable, IND, equal to 1 if a school is an independent and 0 otherwise. The results were

$$\text{ENFORCEMENT} = -24.45 + 29.27\text{CV} - 33.74\text{CV}^2 + 0.52\text{DC}$$
$$(-2.38) \quad (2.16) \quad (-2.15) \quad (2.14)$$
$$+ 8.13\text{SCPOP} + 0.01\text{AGE}$$
$$(2.94) \quad (2.17)$$
$$+ 0.2e - 4\text{STAD} - 0.03 \text{ IND}$$
$$(2.36) \quad (-0.06)$$

IND has a negative but insignificant coefficient. This suggests that independents are monitored carefully in recruiting competition by schools in the areas where they recruit; that is, being an independent adds no useful information to the cartel enforcement process.

In sum, these results support the hypothesis that the NCAA and its member schools use indirect or probabilistic information in order to apprehend violators of the monopsony agreement.

Perennial Winners

An additional question of interest is whether traditional winners are prosecuted at a lower rate. Several variables were used to measure traditional winning, including national television

appearances, mean winning percentage, and top twenty appearances. The results in each case are similar. Below, the results are reported when national television appearances are
added in the estimation of equation (1):

$$\text{ENFORCEMENT} = -25.65 + 24.16\text{CV} - 28.50\text{CV}^2 + 0.50\text{DC}$$
$$(-2.43) \quad (1.77) \quad (-1.87) \quad (2.03)$$
$$+ 8.63\text{SCPOP} + 0.3e - 4\text{STAD} + 0.012\text{AGE}$$
$$(3.07) \quad (2.37) \quad (2.32)$$
$$- 0.20\text{NATTV}$$
$$(-0.83)$$

When measures of traditional winning for a team are added to
equation (1), the probability of NCAA enforcement does not
increase significantly; the other results are basically unchanged. This suggests that NCAA enforcement does not
bother itself with either consistently successful teams or with
teams that never win. If NCAA enforcement were driven by
the desire to detect violations wherever they occur, and winning and violations are positively related, consistent winning
would be, ceteris paribus, an indirect indication of cheating on
the cartel agreement. Nonetheless, consistent winners are no
more likely to be convicted of violations than are consistent
losers. In fact, when the traditional winning measures are used
in place of the coefficient of variation in equation (1), the measures have a marginally negative effect upon enforcement.
This suggests that consistent winners may be prosecuted at a
lower rate than other schools. In support of this result at a
more descriptive level, appendix 2 displays the number of
times each school in our sample has been in the final top
twenty teams over the 1953–83 period and whether or not they
have been put on probation. The teams appearing in the final
top twenty the most often are not the most heavily sanctioned.
It is the teams that have more variable records that are sanctioned more, a result which suggests that the NCAA enforcement process favors perennial football powers.

A Closer Look at Probation

The level of aggregation of the logit analysis obscures two features of NCAA enforcement that are of interest. First, does variation in winning percentage lead *directly* to enforcement? Second,

is enforcement *effective*, that is, does it cost the school success on the playing field? In other words, what can be said about NCAA enforcement with respect to an improving team hypothesis?

In figure 2 the mean winning percentage of detected violators, running from five years prior to the start of probation (t) to five years after, is plotted. The winning percentages of these schools increased, on average, over the five years prior to probation and one year into probation. The latter result is plausible because illegally acquired recruits will continue to impact team quality during the early part of a probation. One year after probation begins, the average winning percentage of detected violatorsstarts to decline and continues to decline through year $t + 4$.

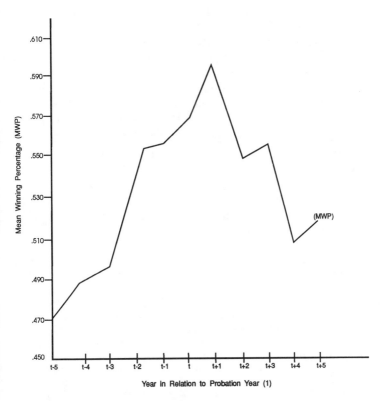

FIGURE 2
Winning Percentage of NCAA Violators

Some recovery from the effects of probation is evident during the fifth season after the sanctions were put into effect.

Table 18 summarizes the changes in mean winning percentages for the teams placed on probation and those that have not been punished by the NCAA. Overall, the mean winning percentage of detected violators increased by more than 12 percentage points from $t - 5$ to $t + 1$. The change in winning percentage over this interval is significant at the 1 percent level and represents an approximately 26 percent increase in the winning percentage of the teams put on probation. Crime pays. By comparison (see bottom of table 18), the average six-year change in mean winning percentage for schools not placed on probation is -0.0015 percent.[8] The difference between the six-year change in mean winning percentage for the two groups of schools is significant at the 5 percent level.

The data for the postsanction years ($t + 1$ to $t + 4$) suggest that enforcement actions decrease the mean winning percentages of detected violators. Over this period the mean winning percentage of detected violators falls by almost 8 percentage points. This decrease is significant at the 5 percent level. It is also different from the mean of the three-year change in winning percentage for no-probation schools at the 5 percent level. Thus, for a team that goes 8–3 in year $t + 1$, probation will, on average, lead to a 7–4 record in subsequent seasons. The addition of one game to a team's loss column may not seem important, but the difference between 8–3 and 7–4 is substantial in terms of bowl games, television appearances, recruiting, and national ranking.[9]

8. The calculations for the no-probation schools are derived as follows. WINPCT is the average winning percentage of all schools in the sample not placed on NCAA probation. WINPCT$_{-1}$ is generated by taking the average of the one-year lag of year-to-year winning percentages for each of these schools. WINPCT$_{-2}$ and so on are derived in the same way, and thus (WINPCT − WINPCT$_{-1}$) and so on are self-explanatory.

9. As an example, take the Oklahoma football program, which was placed on probation by the NCAA for the years 1989 and 1990. For 1989, the Sooners were ineligible for television and postseason appearances. For 1990, the Sooners were ineligible for postseason bowl games. It was estimated that Oklahoma could lose $5 million the first year and $3 million the following year due to their violations. Because of revenue-sharing agreements, the Big Eight, of which Oklahoma is a member, also stood to lose revenue as a result of Oklahoma's probation.

TABLE 18
Changes in Mean Winning Percentage Based on NCAA Enforcement Actions

Probation

$t-5$ to $t+1$	Mean	S.D.	$t+1$ to $t+5$	Mean	S.D.
$WINPCT_{t+1} - WINPCT_{t-5}$	.1231	.266	$WINPCT_{t+4} - WINPCT_{t+1}$	−.0795	.290
$WINPCT_{t-4} - WINPCT_{t-5}$	.0163	.231	$WINPCT_{t+2} - WINPCT_{t+1}$	−.0485	.271
$WINPCT_{t-3} - WINPCT_{t-5}$	.0067	.226	$WINPCT_{t+3} - WINPCT_{t+2}$	−.0075	.257
$WINPCT_{t-2} - WINPCT_{t-4}$	.0574	.244	$WINPCT_{t+4} - WINPCT_{t+3}$	−.0313	.133
$WINPCT_{t-1} - WINPCT_{t-3}$	.0063	.229	$WINPCT_{t+5} - WINPCT_{t+4}$	−.0295	.208
$WINPCT_{t} - WINPCT_{t-2}$	.0171	.271			
$WINPCT_{t+1} - WINPCT_{t}$	.0204	.186			

No Probation

	Mean	S.D.		Mean	S.D.
$WINPCT - WINPCT_{-1}$	−.0009	.020	$WINPCT - WINPCT_{-4}$	−.0001	.028
$WINPCT - WINPCT_{-2}$	−.0017	.024	$WINPCT - WINPCT_{-5}$	−.0002	.024
$WINPCT - WINPCT_{-3}$	−.0013	.029	$WINPCT - WINPCT_{-6}$	−.0015	.025

Recidivists

Three schools in our data were repeat offenders (Houston, Kansas, and Southern Methodist). In general, the results for recidivists are the same as before. Upward variability leads to probation and then to poorer performance with a lag. More specifically, figures 3, 4, and 5 provide illustrations of the impact of enforcement on the three recidivists. In a simple yet revealing way, these figures support the story of winning variability and enforcement. Such cycles in NCAA enforcement against schools are predictable. One-time offenders will be watched more closely than other schools, especially if they start to win again. The recent discussion by the NCAA of radical penalties for repeat offenders (canceling athletic programs for specified periods) indicates the degree to which the cartel is willing to go to suppress the rise of new football powers. Indeed, there has been more than discussion. As mentioned previously, the NCAA dismantled the SMU football program.

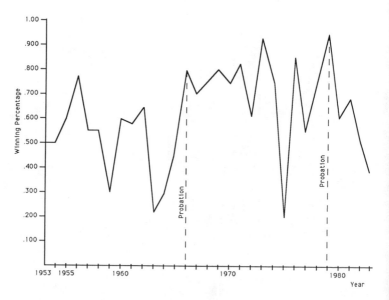

FIGURE 3
NCAA Repeat Offenders: University of Houston

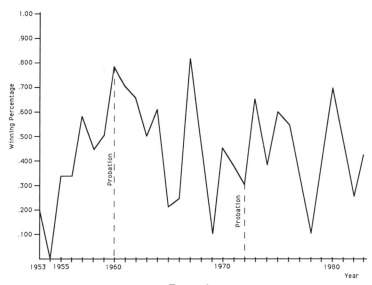

FIGURE 4
NCAA Repeat Offenders: University of Kansas

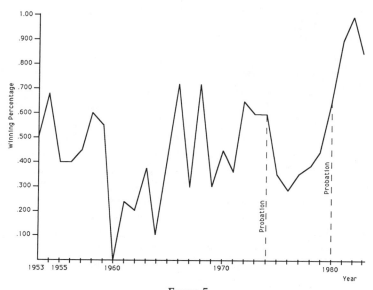

FIGURE 5
NCAA Repeat Offenders: Southern Methodist University

Contrasts in Enforcement

The logit model and descriptive statistics paint a consistent picture of the differential impact of NCAA enforcement policies. In addition to this evidence, a wealth of anecdotal evidence supports the same conclusion. For those who believe that statistical methods are intended to hide rather than clarify reality, these particular episodes provide a sort of common-sense case for the enforcement theory.

Contrasting various enforcement actions by the NCAA may be the best way to present this evidence.[10] The most insightful case occurred several years ago. Ohio State (a traditional power in college athletics with strong ties to long-time NCAA executive director Walter Byers) was found to have given cash gifts and outside aid to athletes in the mid-1950s. Moreover, the Ohio State football coach, Woody Hayes, was alleged to have conducted a continuing loan fund for athletes. In 1956, the school received only an official "reprimand" from the NCAA. In contrast, during the mid-1960s, Illinois operated an almost identical fund for athletes. In spite of self-reporting its violations and being a first-time offender, Illinois received a major, two-year penalty. Curiously enough, Illinois won the Big Ten title two years after starting the secret fund. Later, in the mid-1970s, Michigan State received three years' probation and reduced television appearances for the same type of infraction.

The dominant power in college basketball during much of the 1960s and 1970s, UCLA, was found guilty of certain infractions in the mid-1970s. The violations included cosigning of loans and erroneous eligibility certification. (Additionally, it later became close to common knowledge that alumni support of athletes had been rampant at UCLA during its winning years.) In spite of direct monetary infractions and fraudulent behavior, UCLA received only a reprimand and a minor, one-year probationary period. Over the same general period, the NCAA found Western Kentucky University and other Ohio Valley Conference schools guilty of a number of serious violations. In 1973, Western Kentucky received two years' probation with no television appearances allowed; in 1974, the NCAA

10. This evidence is from the U.S. House hearings, table on enforcement actions, and Jenkins (1967).

placed the entire conference on probation. Again, it is interesting to note the timing of these sanctions. Western Kentucky made it to the NCAA Final Four in 1971, placing third and, en route, soundly defeated one of the dominant powers in NCAA basketball and its in-state rival, the University of Kentucky.

The Southwest Conference during the mid-1980s provides an example of more recent intracartel struggles. Almost all the schools in the conference found themselves on some type of probation, the major exception being the University of Arkansas, a traditional football power. Also, although the University of Texas was placed on probation, its penalty essentially amounted to only a one-year restriction on off-campus recruiting. This resulted in spite of rumors that a Texas tailback was driving a new BMW. In contrast, SMU received the "death penalty" for cash gifts and numerous other violations. Even more telling, Texas Christian University received a multiyear probation, had to repay about $800,000 in revenues, and had its new scholarships drastically cut. The NCAA levied this penalty even though Texas Christian was not a repeat offender, it self-reported its violations, and it suspended several players for almost half of the season when the violations were discovered. SMU rose to prominence in the conference in the late 1970s and early 1980s, finishing in the top three in the nation in 1983. Texas Christian enjoyed its most successful season in decades the year prior to its being investigated.

Finally, consider the NCAA's defense of its enforcement process. One defense used in the 1978 congressional hearings centers on the supposed breadth of NCAA enforcement actions. At the hearings the NCAA supplied a list of enforcement actions which purported to show that the large, traditional powers were punished along with the lesser powers. The case of Kentucky illustrates the weakness of this defense. Kentucky did receive basketball sanctions in 1989, but only after a long and documented history of violations. In addition, the sanctions levied against the traditional powers have often amounted to a harmless slap on the wrist, as table 19 shows. It presents the NCAA's own list from the congressional hearings and separates out several enforcement actions against six of the traditional powers. This list includes the Ohio State penalty discussed earlier. This evidence reinforces the argument that,

TABLE 19

Enforcement Actions against Six Traditional Athletic Powers

Institution, Year	Violations	Penalty
Ohio State, 1956	Outside aid to athletes, cash gifts; improper inducements	Reprimand
North Carolina, 1961	Excessive entertainment of prospects; outside aid	1 year probation*
Texas, 1965	Excessive entertainment of prospects, plus cash and meals	1 year probation*
Arkansas, 1965	Entertainment infractions; inducements; out-of-season practice	1 year probation*
Notre Dame, 1953	Football/basketball tryouts; coach signing and providing grant-in-aid forms	Reprimand
Alabama, 1964	Improper conduct	Reprimand

*No television restrictions.

while enforcement actions may proceed against the college athletic powerhouses, they hardly fall into the category of major penalties.

One particular school requires special consideration. Some may question our theory on the basis of what happened at the University of Oklahoma. Although this school is a perennial winner and has been among the top revenue generators since about 1970, it has found itself on the receiving end of the NCAA enforcement process several times. Is Oklahoma an anomaly? Even though it is a large revenue producer, Oklahoma fits the enforcement theory put forward. In terms of the post–Sanity Code period, Oklahoma is an "up and comer." It has belonged to a conference, the Big Eight, which was originally targeted as a noncomplying conference. Moreover, even in its region, Oklahoma is a new entrant in big-time football. As late as the mid-1950s, the Southwest Conference denied Oklahoma's request for admission. Also, as Oklahoma grew in power and prestige, a well-publicized feud developed in the 1970s between the coaches at arch-rival Texas and those at

Oklahoma. Much of the animosity grew out of the large number of Texas high school players who chose to play at Oklahoma. For such reasons, Oklahoma can be seen as a maverick school in the NCAA, which has, however, been successful in spite of the NCAA's efforts to keep it down.

3. Concluding Remarks

This chapter draws from the model of enforcement outlined in chapter 2 and tests a theory concerning the methods that the NCAA and its member schools use to detect violations of its monopsony agreement. This process is guided by the use of probabilistic evidence. The cartel infers and investigates illegal practices by individual schools by looking at their athletic performances on the field. Much variability of performance leads to suspicion and enforcement. The results also suggest that the enforcement of NCAA rules and regulations has a redistributive impact. Teams with consistently high winning records are not prosecuted more than other teams, even though consistent winning could also be interpreted as an indirect signal that violations are taking place. This fact, coupled with the result that teams with volatile winning records are prosecuted more heavily, suggests that up and coming teams (new entrants to the ranks of the winners) are turned in and set up for probation by consistent winners.

In drawing the inference that NCAA enforcement activities benefit the perennial football powers at the expense of up and coming teams, the authors are not suggesting that most or all of the member schools engage in illegal recruiting practices but that only a few are ever substantially penalized. An alternative interpretation of the evidence we have considered is that the major college football programs, such as those of Alabama, Michigan, Notre Dame, Ohio State, and Penn State, have developed such strong winning traditions over the years that cheating may not be required for them to maintain their dominant position. These schools are able to attract superior high school athletes season after season at the cartel wage with the offer of a package of complementary inputs. Their well-equipped training facilities, quality coaching staffs, talented teammates, national television and media exposure, and so on, increase the present value of an amateur football player's

future professional income relative to the value added by historically weaker programs. Given this factor, along with NCAA
rules that mandate a uniform wage across member schools yet
allow for differences in capital stocks, the traditional football
powers have a built-in competitive advantage in recruiting
the best athletes. Accordingly, the traditional nonpowers—
Clemson, Colorado, Oklahoma, Texas A&M, Texas Christian,
and Minnesota, for instance—have an incentive to break the
cartel rules if they are ever to achieve gridiron success.

Although our empirical analysis does not distinguish between these two alternative views of the world, it is worth
pointing out that NCAA enforcement activities have the same
effect in both cases. Whether the observed pattern of sanctions
is due to the fact that the NCAA has turned a blind eye to the
violations of some of its members but not others or to the fact
that only some members have actually violated the rules is
irrelevant to the conclusion that NCAA enforcement activities
have served to maintain the status quo, benefiting the perennial football powers at the expense of their rivals.

SIX

NCAA Academic Requirements as Barriers to Entry

T wo of the more controversial rules passed by the NCAA in recent times are the requirement of minimum scores on college entrance examinations by potential college athletes (known originally as Proposition 48) and the prohibition on offering scholarships to incoming freshmen declared "partial qualifiers" under Proposition 48 (known as Proposition 42). The story of the enacting of these two rules by the NCAA was outlined in chapter 3. The strongest criticism of Propositions 48 and 42 has centered on the racially biased consequences of the academic requirements; many more blacks than whites have failed to meet the minimum scores.[1]

There are essentially two competing explanations of Proposition 48. NCAA executives and the representatives of member

1. In a recent survey by the NCAA, in which 206 Division I institutions participated, the number of partial qualifiers in all sports was found to have increased between 1987 and 1988. A partial qualifier is ineligible in the first year of college to participate in his or her chosen sport. In 1988, of the schools that participated in the survey, 562, or 5.1 percent, of their freshman athletes were classified as partial qualifiers. This is an increase from 4.5 percent in 1987. In terms of the racial breakdown of the data, 97.8 percent of white freshmen were deemed qualifiers in 1988 while only 85.5 percent of black freshmen were eligible. Of those blacks who were partial qualifiers or nonqualifiers (14.5 percent), 66 percent were categorized as such because they failed to achieve the minimum score of 700 on the SAT. Another 19 percent did not score the minimum SAT score and did not attain the required 2.0 grade point average in the core curriculum (*NCAA News*, March 15, 1989, pp. 1–2).

schools claim that this type of rule promotes the academic life of athletes both at the high school and at the college level; that is, the rule has a public-interest rationale. Others have questioned this explanation on the basis that disqualified athletes lose a year of eligibility even if they demonstrate the ability to pass college course work. This chapter seeks an alternative explanation of such eligibility rules; it asks if a self-interest explanation of the requirements exists.

These restrictions would not be the first historical instance of the adoption of eligibility requirements that benefited some athletes and teams at the expense of others. The history of amateur eligibility rules is replete with instances of interathlete or interorganizational rent seeking. Baker (1982) and Goff, Shughart, and Tollison (1988) survey this history. In fact, many of the early codes of amateurism explicitly revealed their entry-barring intent. A clear example of exclusion is seen in a British footracing rule of 1866 which excluded any individual who played for direct reimbursement or who made his living through manual labor. From the inception of the modern Olympics, some upper-class events such as fencing have allowed "professionals" to compete, while other events have maintained strict amateur rules, as in the famous Jim Thorpe episode, where he had to return his Olympic gold medal, because of having previously been paid a trivial sum to play some professional football games.

Throughout the NCAA's history, some of the support of/opposition to higher academic standards and financial aid restrictions has been motivated by considerations that are not educational. For example, in the mid-1960s the NCAA passed a rule that became known as the "1.6 rule." This rule required athletes to maintain at least a 1.6 grade point average to maintain eligibility. The schools that one might think would have proposed such a rule (e.g., the Ivy League schools) vehemently opposed it.[2] Support came from some of the traditional football powers, such as the Big Ten Conference. Whether or not the support/opposition presents a paradox in this case, it is difficult to reconcile both positions with a public-minded,

2. See Jenkins (1966) for more details on this particular controversy. In general, the Ivy League schools wanted each school to set its own academic policy.

education-first motive. Another example occurred during the Sanity Code period of the late 1940s and early 1950s. As a whole, the Southeastern Conference, Southwest Conference, and Southern Conference (predecessor of the Atlantic Coast Conference) opposed the code, claiming it was biased against the growing southern schools. Among these conferences, the opposition to the code was not limited to particular "outlaw" universities with marginal academic reputations. For instance, the University of Virginia was one of the earliest and most outspoken critics of the code. Again, whether the supporters or detractors or both represent examples of self-seeking behavior, at least one side must not have been pursuing goals that were strictly educational.

The list of such examples could be extended to include minimum sports participation requirements, the "five-year clock" rule, and others. To consider every case would deviate from the primary objective of this chapter, which is to test a self-interest or cartel model of support for stricter eligibility requirements by NCAA member schools based on the model developed in chapter 2. The attempt here is to step beyond the rhetoric about academics and ask whether the votes of schools in favor of stricter academic rules are a direct outcome of variables related to those schools' self-interest on the playing field and hence at the box office? Analyzed specifically are votes by NCAA member schools concerning proposals to trade off an athlete's college entrance examination scores against that athlete's high school grade point average and to limit scholarships on the basis of this trade-off. Several logit models of support of and opposition to these issues are developed and tested.

1. Empirical Model

The theoretical model developed in chapter 2 made a straightforward prediction concerning NCAA entry barriers, especially with respect to academic restrictions on players. Schools with academic brand-name capital and self-imposed academic restrictions gain additional rents if they can successfully put some of the same restrictions on the athletes of all schools. On this basis, among the colleges fielding major football and basketball teams, relatively greater support for new restrictions is expected to come from the institutions with higher academic standards. This is the foundation for the following empirical analysis of Propositions 48 and 42.

This theoretical prediction concerning academics and eligibility rules forms the basis of a general empirical model of support of/opposition to stricter eligibility:

SUPPORT/OPPOSITION = f (ACADEMIC QUALITY, DEMAND FOR ATHLETICS, CARTEL RULE BREAKING, INDEPENDENT AFFILIATION).

As stated previously, higher-quality schools will be more likely to vote for stricter eligibility rules because such schools have a comparative advantage in recruiting academically talented athletes. The eligibility rules allow the more academically oriented schools to impose stricter entrance requirements on other schools.[3] Tighter rules thus increase the competitiveness of higher-quality schools on the playing field. It should also be noted that the individual institution is not the only relevant unit of analysis of whether a school supports or opposes eligibility rules. The importance of the stance of the conference as a whole is seen in the opposition to the Sanity Code by the Southeastern, Southwest, and Southern Conferences, as well as in the Ivy League's opposition to the 1.6 rule.

The condition of ceteris paribus must be invoked. First, the level of demand for athletics at a school will influence the support for tighter eligibility rules. Schools with a high demand for sports will suffer significant revenue losses if athletic success is diminished by stricter eligibility rules. A low-demand school will therefore have a relatively higher demand

3. In fact, if the general student population were required to maintain the Proposition 48 standards, almost 30 percent of the freshman classes at some institutions would not be eligible. Proposition 48 actually derives from an incident at the University of Georgia. A teacher filed a lawsuit claiming that Georgia was going easy on its student athletes. The local embarrassment (loss of brand-name capital?) led the coach, Vince Dooley, to propose higher academic standards for the entire Southeastern Conference. This proposal was adopted by the presidents of these universities. Then, finding itself at a competitive disadvantage relative to other conferences and schools in recruiting, Georgia and the Southeastern Conference led the fight in the NCAA for Proposition 48.

for stricter rules and will be more likely to vote accordingly. Second, some schools have historically engaged in more cartel rule-breaking behavior than other schools (or at least they have been caught and penalized more frequently). Schools that already break the cartel rules will not demand stricter rules that make even more of their recruiting conduct illegal. Overt cartel violators will not favor tighter eligibility requirements. Third, a school without a conference affiliation (an "independent") stands to gain relatively more from athletic success on the playing field because it does not have to share athletic revenues with other conference members. Hence, independent schools will not desire stricter rules that infringe on their possibility of athletic success.[4]

What one has, then, is an intracartel struggle for the rents from athletic success. This struggle pits academically successful schools and conferences against schools and conferences where sports reign supreme. This is not the only form that intracartel struggles take in the NCAA, but it is an interesting competition which is worthy of analysis.

The general self-interest incentives lead to the following operational model of votes for and against stricter eligibility rules:

$$\text{VOTE48} = b_0 + b_1 \text{SAT}_s + b_2 \text{SAT}_c + b_3 \text{ENROLLMENT} + b_4 \text{PROBATION} + b_5 \text{INDEPENDENT},$$

where

VOTE	= 1 if a school votes for the SAT-/grade point average trade-off, = 0 if a school votes against such a trade-off;
SAT(school)	= average SAT score of all enrolling freshmen in 1986 by school;
SAT(conference)	= average SAT score for the schools in a conference in 1986 (for independents, it is the average of all independents);
ENROLLMENT	= enrollment by school of full and part-time students in 1986;

4. This prediction is in contrast to the result in chap. 5 where the independent status of a school added no predictive power to the enforcement model.

PROBATION   = 1 if a school has been on NCAA
                     probation over the 1953–83
                     period,
              = 0 otherwise; and
INDEPENDENT = 1 if a school is not aligned with a
                     conference in football,
              = 0 otherwise.

The sample includes 82 of the 800 member schools in the NCAA (see appendix 3). These 82 schools are all Division I-A schools in football. The sample is limited to this group because the main interest here lies in differences in the self-interests of the major athletic programs.[5] These are the same schools included in the empirical analysis of the preceding chapter.

The dependent variable VOTE is the vote by NCAA members in 1986 on an SAT/grade point average trade-off proposal. NCAA members voted on a proposition to implement an SAT requirement for freshman eligibility, but with the provision that an athlete's high school grade point average (GPA) could offset a lower SAT score. For instance, a student with a C average in high school had to obtain at least a 700 on the SAT, while an athlete with a higher GPA and lower SAT score would also have been permitted to play in his freshman year. The provision would have relaxed an earlier proposition that called for the exclusive use of the SAT (or ACT) score in determining freshman eligibility. Thus, a vote for the provision supported looser restrictions and a vote against the provision favored tighter restrictions on incoming freshman players.

Higher-quality schools are proxied by higher SAT scores. Other things equal, schools whose entrants get higher SAT scores are expected to oppose the SAT/GPA trade-off and to push for the stricter rule; SAT is expected to have a negative sign. ENROLLMENT is used as a proxy for the demand for athletics. As this demand increases, the school is more likely to vote for the SAT/GPA sliding scale. ENROLLMENT is expected

5. SAT or ACT data were not available for the University of Texas at El Paso, Texas Christian, Washington State, and New Mexico State. Also, ACT scores are multiplied by 44 to make them comparable in magnitude to SAT scores. No single conversion multiplier exists; this procedure represents a good approximation. A list of school and conference SAT and ACT scores is given in appendix 3 to this volume.

TABLE 20
Descriptive Statistics

Variable	Mean
SAT (school)	1,036
SAT (conference)	1,035
ENROLLMENT	23,244
PROBATION	0.54
INDEPENDENT	0.24
STADIUM	50,881

to have a positive sign. As an alternative measure of demand, one specification was estimated using stadium size in place of ENROLLMENT. PROBATION is a measure of the relative amount of detected cartel-breaking activity by a school. As noted earlier, cartel breakers will not favor stricter rules. A positive sign is expected on PROBATION. Finally, independent schools will benefit relatively more from looser eligibility requirements because these schools do not share football revenues with members of a conference. Independents are expected to favor the SAT/GPA scale, and this implies a positive sign on INDEPENDENT, other things equal.

Table 20 presents the descriptive statistics for the independent variables. Table 21 presents three logit estimations of the model.[6] Specification I includes school SAT without conference SAT, and specification II includes conference SAT without school SAT. This is necessary because of collinearity between these two variables. Specification III uses stadium size rather than enrollment as the measure of the demand for athletics. Overall, the specifications explain between 20 and 40 percent of the likelihood of a vote for or against the SAT/GPA scale when the pseudo-R^2 is calculated.

Specifically, the estimates indicate that SAT scores have a negative impact on likelihood of support for a looser rule. Of the two SAT measures, the conference SAT score has a stronger and more significant coefficient (1 percent level). Higher-quality academics lead to support for stricter rules. The coefficient on ENROLL-MENT is positive and significant at the 1 percent level. Higher

6. Estimates were generated by the LOGIT procedure of Micro TSP.

TABLE 21
LOGIT Analysis of Votes for SAT/GPA Sliding Scale

Variable	Coefficient/(t-statistic)		
	I	II	III
Intercept	−0.25	17.36	15.50
	(0.08)	(2.52)	(2.52)
SAT (school)	−0.0024	—	
	(0.91)	—	
SAT (conference)	—	−0.02	−0.02
	—	(2.94)	(2.70)
ENROLLMENT	1.2e-4	1.4e-4	
	(3.66)	(4.23)	
PROBATION	0.66	0.99	1.19
	(1.19)	(1.65)	(2.17)
INDEPENDENT	1.65	2.33	1.51
	(2.24)	(2.90)	(2.19)
STADIUM SIZE	—	—	2.97e-5
	—	—	(1.82)
Log (likelihood)	−37.55	−32.85	−43.13

Note: Vote for the sliding scale indicates support for looser eligibility requirements.

demand as measured by enrollment leads to support for looser rules. In specification III, the alternative measure of demand, STADIUM SIZE, is positive and significant at the 7 percent level. PROBATION has a positive coefficient that is significant at the 10 percent level in specification II and at the 5 percent level in specification III. Cartel breakers vote against stricter rules. INDEPENDENT has a positive coefficient that is significant at the 5 percent level in specifications I and III and at the 1 percent level in specification II. Independent schools are more likely to vote for looser restrictions, other things equal.

As an additional test of the importance of academic reputation in support for eligibility rules, votes by schools on Proposition 42 were obtained. As we have seen, this 1988 proposal denies scholarships to athletes failing to meet the full qualifier provisions of Proposition 48. The following model was estimated:

$$\text{VOTE42} = b_0 + b_1 \text{ SAT}_s + b_2 \text{ SAT}_c + b_3 \text{ ENROLLMENT} + b_4 \text{ PROBATION} + b_5 \text{ INDEPENDENT,}$$

where

VOTE42 = 1 if a school votes for denying scholarships,
= 0 if a school votes against denying scholarships.

In this case a vote for the proposal is a vote in support of stricter eligibility requirements. The explanatory variables are expected to have similar effects, but their signs will be reversed because of the switch in the definition of the dependent variable. School and conference SAT scores are expected to have positive signs; ENROLLMENT, PROBATION, INDEPEN-DENT, and STADIUM SIZE are expected to have negative signs.

Table 22 presents the results of logit estimations of support for Proposition 42. The sample of schools is identical to that for the previous estimation of which schools would and would not vote for modification of Proposition 48. The results are similar

TABLE 22
LOGIT Analysis of Votes for Proposition 42

Variable	Coefficient/(t-Statistic)		
	I	II	III
Intercept	−2.18	−6.95	−6.86
	(0.79)	(1.21)	(1.23)
SAT (school)	−0.003	—	
	(1.52)	—	
SAT (conference)	—	0.008	0.008
	—	(1.54)	(1.46)
ENROLLMENT	−5.37e-5	−6.49e-5	
	(2.23)	(2.63)	
PROBATION	0.14	−0.03	−0.22
	(0.29)	(0.06)	(0.44)
INDEPENDENT	−0.51	−0.73	−0.56
	(0.87)	(1.18)	(0.94)
STADIUM SIZE	—	—	−1.80e-5
	—	—	(1.27)
Log (likelihood)	−46.69	−46.63	−49.77

Note: Vote for Proposition 42 indicates support for stricter eligibility require-ments.

to those found for the Proposition 48 vote, given, of course, the expected sign reversals. Generally, however, these results are not as strong as are those for the vote on the sliding scale. School SAT scores are not significant at any level. Conference SAT scores are positive and significant at the 13 percent level. Enrollment shows the most stability across tables 21 and 22; it is negative and significant at the 5 percent level.

The effects of other variables were also estimated. The volatility of winning record, an alternative measure of cartel breaking, does not have a significant impact on support for looser rules, nor does historical winning percentage. The interaction of conference and school SAT scores has a negative and significant effect on votes.

2. Concluding Remarks

Some evidence in support of the idea that NCAA votes on academic rules such as Propositions 48 and 42 are not entirely guided by the idea of improving the educational quality of student athletes is presented in this chapter. While our results do not disprove the presence of a racial bias behind these rules, the results support an alternative explanation: schools are pursuing their competitive self-interest. Nonetheless, Propositions 48 and 42 work like entry barriers whether they were conceived as such or not. It happens that in this case a particular racial group, blacks, have borne the brunt of the restrictions. In the past, other groups have suffered because of eligibility rules; for instance, most southern schools and their athletes suffered as a result of the Sanity Code restrictions of the mid-century. The evidence also indicates that the restrictions are not strictly education-oriented; virtually all of the athletes declared ineligible by Proposition 48 subsequently qualified to play for their respective schools. Was the year off the reason for these athletes' academic success? Perhaps to some degree it was. But the best guess is that Proposition 48 did not greatly alter the study habits of student athletes. Rather, it simply denied a year of competition to a group of athletes who showed they could pass college courses.

SEVEN

Capture of the NCAA Regulatory Process

O nce in the hands of the NCAA, an alleged violation is investigated by the NCAA staff and a report is made to the relevant internal committees. It is the work of these committees to decide innocence or guilt and the degree of punishment. These internal committees are manned by representatives from NCAA member schools. Because the committee representatives are primarily agents of their institutions, their decisions will not be divorced from the underlying competitive struggle for larger shares of the cartel rents. Instead, members will attempt to gain differential shares through the operation of these committees.

This chapter draws on some of the basic points made in chapter 2 about the distribution of cartel rents in order to explain more fully the capture of the NCAA regulatory process. The basic point is straightforward. Schools with substantial reputational and physical assets have an advantage in capturing the NCAA enforcement apparatus. This advantage dates from the institution of the modern cartel rules around 1950. In effect, these schools grandfathered themselves into control of the enforcement process and over time have remained in control of the NCAA committees. Among other things, this implies that committee membership will be a function of historical winning percentage, all else equal, and, moreover, that probationary actions taken by the NCAA will generally be directed against schools which show an improvement in winning percentage and thereby threaten the status and rents of the traditional football powers. In other words, if a school is a traditional winner in college football, it will seek to capture the NCAA enforcement apparatus in order to perpetuate the status quo. We test this hypothesis on the available data for membership of schools on the primary NCAA enforcement body—the NCAA Council.[1]

Section 1 spells out the capture argument in more detail and attempts to answer some questions concerning the hypothesis. Section 2 tests the capture theory for college football programs. Section 3 offers some concluding remarks.

1. Capture and NCAA Structure

As outlined in chapters 3 and 4, the enforcement structure of the NCAA has varied little since its inception in 1952. On an operational basis the final regulatory power of the organization resides in the NCAA Council, which is composed of elected officials from member schools. Candidates for Council positions are proposed by a nominating committee or by nominations from the floor at the annual NCAA convention. The size and membership of the Council have varied over time. (Membership data are given in appendix 4 near the end of this volume.) Over the 1952–77 period, the Council basically conducted enforcement procedures or served as a court of last resort for enforcement appeals. At different times over this period, the Council was assisted by a Committee on Infractions, composed almost exclusively of a subcommittee of Council members. The Committee on Infractions was assisted in its work by the (relatively small) internal NCAA staff. Over the 1952–73 period, the Committee on Infractions reported its findings to the Council and the Council decided on penalties. From 1973 to the present, the Committee on Infractions has investigated and imposed penalties for violations, with the Council serving as a court of appeals. The Committee on Infractions is appointed by the NCAA Council.

As stressed earlier, the NCAA is a private regulatory institution.[2] What this chapter examines is the degree to which and

---

1. See U.S. House of Representatives (1978) and Falla (1981).

2. See *National Collegiate Athletic Association, Petitioner, v. Jerry Tarkanian*, 87-1061 (Supreme Court of the United States), especially pp. 13–20, where the Supreme Court concluded that the NCAA is not a "state actor" but a private organization.

how this regulatory apparatus might be "captured" by certain member schools. Generally, in the capture theory of regulation, the regulators (such as governmental agencies and boards) are distinct from the industry that they regulate, at least in their preregulatory careers (Stigler 1975; Eckert 1981), and their interests are subverted to the interests of the regulated industry. In the case of the NCAA, one step in the simple capture theory is obviated: the regulators are drawn from the ranks of the regulated industry. As a private regulatory institution, this cartel was designed to be self-regulating. This aspect of the NCAA cartel actually makes the formulation and testing of a capture hypothesis somewhat easier, since the interests of the *regulators* can be assumed to be largely coincident with those of their *schools*.

Chapter 2 argued that it was reasonable to assume that the ability of a school to obtain rents from cartelization relative to other schools will be linked to its revenue production. Then, with revenue and rent determined by the amount of assets possessed by a school, it can be hypothesized that capture will be a function of these assets. Schools with more reputational capital in athletics, for instance, will have bargaining advantages within the cartel because of the relatively large rents they generate.[3]

When the cartel process was instituted in 1952, the rules were written by the NCAA Council, which was controlled by schools with long traditions of winning in college football. Capture was effected from the outset by these schools, and it has been maintained since that time. Capture of the NCAA enforcement process was a means of rent protection by the traditional winners in college football. These rents accrue from high national rankings, television and bowl appearances, and the other economic advantages of having a winning football team. Such returns are protected by selectively using the enforcement process to punish potential entrants into the ranks of the national football powerhouses. In other words, when a school starts to *improve* its winning percentage, an NCAA in-

3. At this point it is important to reemphasize an earlier point. The NCAA Council and committees are not simply staffed by coaches and athletic directors. Deans, vice-presidents, law professors, and other faculty are the regulators along with athletic department personnel.

vestigation is likely to be launched, and the school, if it is found in violation of any of a myriad of NCAA rules, is put on probation. Probation takes the form of limiting the ability of the school to share in the above-mentioned rents and to recruit quality athletes with which to maintain its newly found winning ways. In such a way, traditional winners deter and slow down the entry of schools into big-time college football.

The historical record for the 1947–52 period paints this picture very clearly. The movement toward the modern eligibility and output restraints benefited and was pushed by certain schools and conferences relative to others. The Big Ten and eastern schools lobbied for the restraints over the objections of mainly southern schools, especially schools from the Southeastern Conference, the Southwest Conference, and the Southern Conference (now the Atlantic Coast Conference). In the days of the Sanity Code and the subsequent, longer-lasting agreements, the schools which felt the impact of sanctions which were adopted were primarily from the Big Eight Conference (Kansas and Oklahoma State) and the Border Conference (Arizona, New Mexico, Texas Tech, and so on). In some cases, entire conferences (such as the Border Conference and later the Ohio Valley Conference) were sanctioned.[4]

This is not to suggest that a dynamic element does not exist with respect to capture of the process. The "haves" and "have nots" change over long periods of time. For example, Texas, North Carolina, Alabama, Georgia, Arkansas, Tennessee, and other schools are now certainly part of the upper echelon of the NCAA, while some of the successful schools of the 1940s and 1950s have faded, such as Rice, TCU, and SMU. Upon a close inspection of the basis of these dynamic changes, our primary point remains intact. The southern schools which are now part of the mainstream (1) were by and large already successful by the 1950s; (2) possessed large quantities of physical assets and the ability to increase these assets substantially; and (3) were large public universities with large alumni pools. In contrast, the schools which have faded are small, private universities with, typically, higher academic standards.

---

4. See Lawrence (1982, 1987) for the relevant historical details.

The point about the impact of NCAA enforcement on recruiting is important because it indicates how schools are able to maintain control of the relevant rents over a long period of time. An enforcement action against a school directly limits its recruiting ability through the limitation of scholarships and so forth. It also indirectly affects recruiting by limiting television and bowl appearances and thereby limiting the ability of the school to attract high-quality secondary school athletes. As the ability of a school to recruit and hence to win declines after it is put on probation, the allocation of high school players across colleges is further impacted. Moreover, in the long run a "multiplier" effect is generated as funds for large capital projects are allocated by legislators and boosters and as reputations are established. Losing leads to less support along these margins. Without many of these assets (that are fixed in the short run) or the winning reputations to attract the funds to augment these assets, and without pecuniary means to attract athletes, the new entrant returns to its losing ways and the rents of the traditional winners are protected.

Note that this theory of capture implies that not all schools have to cheat on the cartel. The traditional winners can maintain their status without cheating. By identifying and penalizing potential entrants that are paying players in excess of the NCAA guidelines, such schools are made relatively less attractive to high school athletes. The traditional winners already have a stock of brand-name capital associated with their program that translates into more national exposure, more resources devoted to football training, more bowl trips, and the like. They thus are able to recruit high-quality players without making explicit side payments to them. If a school attempts to break this recruiting lock of the major schools by making side payments to players, it is put on probation in order to maintain the recruiting advantage of the major schools. In such a way the major schools can remain both "clean" and in control of the cartel over time so as to protect their football rents. The potential entrants are prevented from making the investment expenditures necessary to build their reputational capital. Nor should one conclude that the capture theory implies that "cheating" in the NCAA must involve blatant violations. The rules are diverse and detailed so that schools can be put on probation for the most trivial of activities. Schools do not have to make outright payments to be put on probation. The major schools can keep their advantages intact by punishing potential entrants by piling up petty, technical violations.[5]

The potential for logrolling raises an issue for the capture theory. A school need not have direct representation on the NCAA Council in order to sway regulatory decisions. Capture can be effected indirectly, much as it can in regular politics with interest groups supplying votes and money to particular candidates. This aspect of how the NCAA works makes testing the capture theory more difficult since schools which have never been Council members clearly have avenues by which to influence Council decisions. Two points are worth noting here. First, the NCAA has adopted rules which encourage schools to vote on items of direct interest to their institutions. Also, different committees serve the various levels of NCAA schools. Second, direct representation seems more efficient than indirect representation in this case since Council members represent schools and are not simply specialists in representation who go about seeking votes and other types of support in exchange for future favors.

In any event, the primary contours of this theory of NCAA capture are clear. Control of the regulatory process will be sought by schools that are perennial winners in college football.

2. Evidence

The evidence on the capture hypothesis is presented in two parts. First, a logit model is developed using data on eighty schools to test whether membership on the NCAA Council is influenced by a school's historical winning percentage and prior sanctions, holding other factors constant. Second, a more disaggregate and descriptive statistical look at membership on the NCAA Council is presented. The main interest here is in committee membership by schools which are widely recog-

5. For example, at the 1978 congressional hearings, Mississippi State University contended that the main piece of hard evidence against the school when it was placed on major probation was that a player had received a discount on clothes worth about $10.

nized as some of the more successful programs in college athletics. In both cases, membership on the NCAA Council is taken as a good measure of the ability to influence outcomes, especially in the enforcement process.

Logit Analysis

From data sources (e.g., U.S. House of Representatives 1978; Falla 1981), measures of the variables of central interest are derived. First, the man-years of membership by school on the NCAA Council can be measured. Second, whether a school's sports program has been placed on probation can be determined. Finally, the mean winning percentage by school is available. The theory suggests that membership on the Council qua enforcement committee will be a positive function of a school's mean winning percentage in football, all else equal. Our sample consists of eighty-two big-time NCAA football powers, the same group as in the previous chapters.[6]

To test the theory, the following model was specified;

$$\text{MEMBERSHIP} = b_0 + b_1 \text{WINPCT} + b_2 \text{PROB} + b_3 \text{AGE} + b_4 \text{AGE2} + b_5 \text{LIBRARY}, \tag{1}$$

where

MEMBERSHIP	= 1 if a school was a member of the NCAA Council, 1952–77;
WINPCT	= a school's mean winning percentage in football, 1953–83;
PROB	= the fitted values from an instrumental equation (see footnote 7);
AGE	= founding date of school;
AGE2	= founding date of school squared; and
LIBRARY	= bound volumes in school library, 1987.

As discussed above, we expect a positive sign on WINPCT. After getting representation on the enforcement committee,

6. The membership model does not include all schools in the NCAA (all of which may sit on the Council), only the schools with major football programs for which all of the relevant data were available.

winning schools use this power to secure their status quo position as winners. Probation is treated as endogenous to membership on the NCAA Council. Therefore, PROB is the fitted value from an instrumental equation.[7] PROB can be thought of as an entry barrier. The greater the improvement in a school's winning record, the more likely it is that that school will be placed on probation. In other words, NCAA enforcement actions are used for the benefit of traditional winners at the expense of up-and-coming schools. AGE proxies for a grandfathering process in NCAA regulation. Older schools are more likely to have had greater influence in the formation and subsequent control of NCAA activities. AGE should carry a negative sign. AGE2, the square of the founding date of the school, controls for a possible diminishing effect of school age on membership. Finally, LIBRARY is entered as a hedonic measure of school quality. If high-quality schools have less incentive to cheat on the cartel because of alternative means of establishing and maintaining their brand names, they may seek Council membership in order to protect their general competitive position. High-quality schools are expected to invest in reputational capital, and one way to protect their investment is to capture a seat on the NCAA Council. We expect a positive sign on LIBRARY.

The results of estimating equation (1) by logit are shown in table 23. All variables explaining MEMBERSHIP are significant at the 10 percent level or better. The mean winning percentage of a school, WINPCT, has the expected positive sign and is significant at the 5 percent level. The greater the mean winning percentage, the greater the probability a school is able to capture a seat on the NCAA Council. This result is consistent with the capture theory. PROB has the expected negative sign and is significant at the 5 percent level. Those schools placed on probation are less likely to be members of the NCAA Council, ceteris paribus. The founding date of a school, AGE and AGE^2,

7. The instrumental equation is as follows:

$$PROB = -20.62 + 4.42\ CV + .012\ AGE,$$
$$(-1.55)\quad (2.06)\qquad (1.69)$$

where CV is the coefficient of variation of a school's winning percentage. The numbers in parentheses are t-statistics.

TABLE 23
LOGIT Estimate of Membership

Independent Variable	Coefficient/ t-Statistic
Constant	1047.4*
	(1.68)
WINPCT	.0068**
	(2.12)
PROB (predicted)	−5.42**
	(−2.07)
AGE	−1.16*
	(−1.72)
AGE2	.0003*
	(1.76)
LIBRARY	.0009+
	(3.32)
Log (likelihood)	−44.355
N	82

*significant at the 10 percent level.
**significant at the 5 percent level.
+significant at the 1 percent level.

carry the expected signs and are significant at the 1 percent level. Older schools have a greater probability of capturing a seat on the NCAA Council, though with a diminishing effect. Finally, LIBRARY has the expected sign and is significant at the 1 percent level. All else equal, schools with better academic reputations have a greater probability of being members of the NCAA Council.

Descriptive Statistics

The aggregation in the logit analysis masks some more subtle aspects of committee membership. Alternatively, consider some simple calculations based on the NCAA Council membership data.

In the list of Council membership for 1952–77, Division I-A schools filled a total of 156 slots (each slot is a school-year of Council membership). If school-years of membership were equally divided among the eighty or so Division I-A schools in the data set, each school would have served about two years. A simple question is whether the elite programs serve on the

Council at or above this rough average, which would be implied by a complete equality of membership.

Table 24 reports the results of summing years of Council membership for seven of the most successful football programs, Michigan, Texas, Tennessee, Georgia, Arkansas, Ohio State, and Alabama, as well as one of the most successful basketball programs, North Carolina. As the results show, all of these schools served more than the two-year benchmark. Michigan leads the group with 8 school-years on the Council. In total, these eight schools account for 44 years of the 156 school-years across all Division I-A schools. This is almost 28 percent of the available committee spaces, while these schools account for fewer than 10 percent of all Division I-A programs.

Certainly, there can be anomalies where losing programs served a large number of years. Nonetheless, these results do lend less aggregated support to the logit estimation findings. These eight programs are unarguably among the top fifteen programs over the last forty years or so, and the fact that no one of them served less than three years and the group averages over five years of service is in line with the capture theory of the NCAA.

TABLE 24
NCAA Council Membership of Eight Major
Programs, 1952–77

Institution	Years on Council
Michigan	8
Texas	6
Tennessee	6
Georgia	6
Arkansas	5
North Carolina	5
Ohio State	4
Alabama	3
Total	43*

*This is out of 156 total years for all Division I-A schools.

3. Concluding Remarks

The NCAA is a monopsonistic cartel. This chapter argues that it was established and has been operated over time in the interest of perennial college football powers. These schools use membership on the NCAA Council to deter the entry to the ranks of the winners of schools with improving records which threaten the rents of the incumbent winners from such activities as television and bowl appearances. Moreover, the process of capture by the traditional winners in college football maintains their comparative advantage over other schools in recruiting high-quality athletes, thereby maintaining their control of college football over time.

EIGHT

The State of NCAA Policy

The basic conclusion of this study is that the NCAA is a well-functioning cartel with respect to student athletes. Like most cartels, the NCAA faces the problem of competition among member schools for rents, but this only embellishes the basic conclusion. It bears repeating that the study does not seek a normative result. The purpose is not to endorse or castigate NCAA policies. It should also be emphasized that the study does not imply that the NCAA uses the vocabulary of the economic theory of cartels in its meetings. The analysis stands whether the phrase of choice is "eligibility rules" or "entry barriers," "compensation" or "grants-in-aid," "student athlete" or "labor resource." The observable impact, regardless of vocabulary, is control of prices, reduction of output, creation and transfer of rent, and limitations on competition.

The purpose of this chapter is not to make proposals for reform.[1] Instead, the positive analytical approach of the book is maintained to examine the interest (or lack thereof) in reform of the NCAA, the sources of criticism, and some proposed solutions. A central theme in the analysis is the question of why policy critiques and reform proposals never (or very rarely) view the NCAA as a cartel and propose appropriate remedies. The focus is on several sources of policy criticism and reform, including the NCAA itself, sports fans, faculty, the media, players, and the legal system. Lastly, the actions taken at the 1991 NCAA convention, which has been hailed as a "reform convention," and the recommendations of the Knight Commission on the reform of intercollegiate athletics are re-

1. For a short overview of federal government intervention in college athletics, see *New York Times*, October 1, 1989, p. 45.

viewed and assessed in the context of the basic cartel approach to the NCAA taken in this book.

1. Policy and Reform

The NCAA

Policy review and criticism of the NCAA originates in many places. Yet the NCAA itself (meaning the executive staff, committees, institutions, and coaches) serves as an important source of suggestions for change. Because of this, policy proposals and actions rarely, if ever, break out of the cartel framework. In nearly every case of proposed policy change, an identifiable interest group within the NCAA seeking a larger share of the cartel rents serves as the source of the proposal. Instead of real and substantive change, new policies almost always fit neatly into the narrative about intracartel competition.

In fact, previous chapters analyzed several examples of policy changes and proposals which are consistent with the cartel as a whole trying to solve the monopsony problem or with schools seeking a larger share of cartel rents. Certainly, the Proposition 48 and 42 votes did not limit cartel power. Instead, they reduced competition among schools and provided a relatively larger share of rents to schools with higher academic standards. The limitation on the number of visits a high school athlete may make to a campus (financed by the various schools) obviously benefits schools with better reputations. A recruit with only five possible visits is less likely to look at smaller, more obscure schools.[2] Even the Oklahoma-Georgia case that ended the monopoly control of television rights by the NCAA did not arise as an effort to limit cartel power. Instead, it was simply the consequence of larger schools feeling the pinch of redistribution from smaller schools and seeking to recapture a larger share of the rents. Most of the "reforms" initiated by the NCAA, ranging from the Sanity Code to increased sanctions, have at least the impact if not the intent of strengthening the collusive arrangement.

At any rate, looking to the NCAA itself as a source of potential reform of college athletics is equivalent to putting the

2. For a brief discussion of the effects of such a rule on recruiting by smaller schools, see Feinstein (1988, p. 30).

fox in charge of the henhouse. Several recent occurrences amplify this point. At NCAA President's Commission meeting held in October 1989 the usual subjects were discussed for submission to the general membership at the annual convention in January 1990. Although the commission considered banning spring football practice, it compromised and proposed to reduce spring practice by half and eliminate contact drills. For Division I basketball, the commission proposed to delay the start of fall practice by one month to November 15, to push back the first game until December 20 (previously it was the fourth Friday in November), and to reduce the number of games played from twenty-eight to twenty-five. These proposals, stripping away the rhetoric, will reduce costs, restrict output, and increase prices.

In 1990 media attention to scandals, legislative pressures, charges of racial bias, and financial conditions prompted an unusually high interest in NCAA "reform". Because of congressional influence and impending legislation, the NCAA adopted measures to make graduation rates public. The new basketball tournament contract initiated a discussion about revenue sharing. A special NCAA committee suggested a graduation bonus and a player emergency fund. Other voices within the NCAA, such as that of LSU's Dale Brown, called for player stipends. Ultimately, the NCAA decided to disburse funds on the basis of conference-level performance in the tournament in previous years. As mentioned in chapter 3, evolving market conditions have prompted conference realignments in larger numbers than usual.

These developments have attracted a good deal of attention in the sports media. Yet the current reforms fit within the boundaries of cartel theory. To some extent, the locus of bargaining power is shifting toward the conference level, as demonstrated by the ongoing realignments and the tournament revenue distribution plan. This does not lie outside typical cartel behavior. It simply indicates battles among coalitions of schools rather than between individual schools. For example, in 1988 the NCAA rejected a Memphis State University (a highly scrutinized program) plan to help its former players by providing scholarships to those who had not graduated. The NCAA feared that such scholarships would provide an unfair inducement to athletes. In contrast, the tutorial services provided to athletes by some of the NCAA members at significant expense are viewed as evidence of schools that are interested in education.

In addition to adopting reforms which strengthen its cartel power, the NCAA has actively attempted to block more general reforms in amateur athletics in the United States. In doing so, the NCAA has sometimes found itself at odds with other amateur governing bodies. The NCAA carried on a running battle for control of amateur athletics with the Amateur Athletic Union (AAU) dating from the inception of the AAU (Flath 1963). Later, as substantial changes began to occur in U.S. amateur rules and governance in the late 1970s, the NCAA found itself in opposition to the U.S. Olympic Committee (USOC). At the hearings for what became the Amateur Sports Act, Walter Byers, executive director of the NCAA, strongly opposed increasing USOC authority over domestic amateur competition because, as he put it, the USOC is "dominated by international franchise sports interest."[3] Interpreted in the fabric of cartel behavior, the NCAA opposed USOC control because the USOC was moving toward liberalization of eligibility and compensation rules. Prior to this time, U.S. amateur athletes outside NCAA jurisdiction had faced restrictions similar to those faced by athletes within. During the late 1970s and early 1980s, athletes gained the right to accept sizable sums of money for competing as long as a recognized amateur group acted as trustee over the funds allocated to athletes for "living allowances." Clearly, such liberalization within the NCAA is inconsistent with the maintenance of cartel power.

Fans

The interest of the average college sports fan in reform of the NCAA is minimal. This disinterest, though, has its roots in rational behavior rather than lethargy. In view of the Supreme Court decision in the Oklahoma-Georgia case, the televised output markets of the NCAA are relatively competitive. Fans receive large quantities of televised collegiate events at basically competitive prices. In the live attendance market, fans

3. See U.S. Senate (1977).

147

may be subject to price discrimination schemes by their schools, but these in any event are voluntary transactions which do not affect the total number of games available for attendance. In addition, although fans in the aggregate gained from the Supreme Court decision, they did not initiate the case. Any one fan stands to gain such a small amount from taking up the reform banner (even before the case) that the costs of involvement outweigh the benefits. This situation is akin to the rational voting model. Any particular person may choose to vote, but such political involvement must be explained as a result of consumption by the voter or fan rather than because of the direct benefits from becoming involved in the political process through voting.

Faculty

It has been stressed that the NCAA is not just a club of coaches and athletic directors. University executives and some faculty cooperate with and direct athletic personnel. The faculty at the major producers of college sports benefit from the implicit revenue transfers from athletics. Obviously, not all university faculty support NCAA policies or consider themselves beneficiaries of these policies. Some of the most ardent critics of college sports and advocates of reform and/or elimination of modern college athletics are college faculty members. One source of dissatisfaction is philosophical in nature. These faculty do not like the joining of the business aspects of college athletics to other university concerns. Other faculty perceive athletics to be detrimental to the financial welfare of the university's academic units. With small programs this concern may have some foundation, while in other cases it is a misperception of the actual net flow of revenues, as discussed earlier.

The particular proposals for change tend to hover around the reduction of the scale of operation, such as limiting scholarships, movement to a lower division or elimination of a sport, or the entire elimination of intercollegiate athletics. These reformers have made impacts. For instance, after the imposition of the "death penalty," SMU maintained its football program at the Division I-A level but moved its home games from Texas Stadium to its small, on-campus facility. Wichita State (Division I-A) and the University of Texas at

Arlington (Division I-AA), both with struggling and poorly supported football programs, eliminated football.

Elimination of programs by the large producers would have the eventual impact of eliminating the cartel. Such a move appears highly unlikely. In contrast, though, the opposition to big-time college sports by some faculty actually enhances the NCAA's monopsony power. This is because direct payments to players represent an even greater commercialization of athletics in the eyes of some. In addition, faculty concerns about athletic versus academic expenditures, whether justified or not, make explicit payments to players less likely and enhance the transfer of rents from athletes.

Media

The media present a paradox in their treatment of NCAA policy and reform. On the one hand, newspaper and television coverage related to NCAA policies has grown tremendously. Yet almost none of this attention focuses on the cartelization of collegiate sports and its consequences. Most of the coverage deals in a piece-by-piece fashion with institutional problems (secret payments, coaching decisions) or with NCAA propositions in isolation from each other. While many have questioned the wisdom of some policies, the ethics of some personnel, and even the spirit of some of the rules, no systematic thread that ties different episodes together, such as cartel theory, has surfaced. This is in spite of the seeming interest that such a story would generate in the popular media. If there is, for example, a widespread conspiracy or widespread cheating, why would not an enterprising reporter win a Pulitzer Prize by exposing such practices? Why does this paradox exist? What explains the reluctance to investigate the NCAA from a systematic viewpoint as a collusive group of producers operating much like an OPEC (in inputs instead of outputs)?

This is not to say that no critical analyses or reform proposals have been offered by the media. As early as 1930, editorials in campus newspapers and the *New York Times* called for changes such as directly subsidizing athletes or reducing emphasis on athletics.[4] Today, the most persistent critics of college athletic

4. See *New York Times*, November 2 and 7, 1930.

abuses are often found in the media. A recent voice for change was that of Jonathan Yardley (who previously called for the banning of big-time college sports), who wrote a commentary advocating NCAA reform. He saw hope in the form of a new private commission headed by a former president of Notre Dame and the NCAA President's Commission.[5] Yet analogies between the NCAA and other cartels such as OPEC are rarely, if ever, drawn. And, as is the case in Yardley's editorial, it is not recognized that college presidents, just like athletic directors and coaches, have an incentive to maintain the cartel. The main difference is where they desire the cartel proceeds to be spent.

Some might suggest that the reason for any reluctance by the media to pursue a cartel story is that the cartel idea is fiction. This criticism was dealt with in chapter 1. Given the evidence reviewed and presented in this book, if the NCAA is not a collusive organization of schools for economic benefit, then an indefensible alternative is left: the NCAA is filled with a majority of public-interested people who rarely recognize or understand the consequences of their decisions. Given that individuals are generally self-interested and that NCAA policymakers are not dull-minded, this explanation seems inconceivable.

If the cartel theory of the NCAA is accepted, one must turn elsewhere to explain the void in the media on the subject. One explanation may reside in the price that must be paid to write such a story. By this is meant the trade-off that sportswriters face between investigation and access. Coaches control access to themselves, to nonplaying team personnel, and to players. Sportswriters may be hesitant to pursue some lines of investigations because of the possible future ramifications on their ability to cover other stories.[6] In concert with this factor are the perquisites provided the media by some colleges and coaches, such as media facilities and food. Additionally, during the 1978 congressional hearings, one witness testified that a close relationship exists between NCAA investigators and the sports press.[7] The reason seems obvious and akin to the reason for

5. See *Philadelphia Inquirer*, October 11, 1989, p. 11A.

6. See the testimony of Brent Clark in U.S. Senate (1977).

7. A particular example is noted by Feinstein (1986, p. 94) in the case of Indiana basketball. A respected sportswriter for a Bloomington paper maintains close ties with the Indiana coach, Bob Knight. The writer discussed in his

close liaisons between the press and public law enforcement officials or their subordinates elsewhere. The sports reporter receives tips and up-to-date information while the NCAA investigator also picks up valuable information on what is going on in college athletics, as well as favorable press coverage. Noting that incentives exist for sportswriters to establish close ties with the NCAA does not indicate that sportswriters are not interested in accurate stories. Sportswriters, though, are economic agents who respond to incentives like everyone else.

While personal incentives may have something to do with the lack of media investigation of the NCAA as a cartel, there is evidence to suggest that personal incentives alone cannot explain the general reluctance of the media to report along cartel lines. Several regional papers—for example, the *Lexington Herald-Leader* and the *Dallas Morning News*—have risked access to break stories of "scandal" within college athletics. Also, an ever-increasing number of books have set out to expose some of the problems in college athletics. If a willingness exists to investigate and print these stories, what is the reason for the lack of a systematic investigation of the NCAA as a cartel?

One alternative explanation is implied by the *Lexington Herald-Leader/Dallas Morning News* cases. The media in these instances and others are coopted into the enforcement process and actually serve as an additional monitor for the NCAA. Again, this does not imply collusion between the NCAA and the media. Instead, the cooperation in enforcement may be completely coincidental. By and large, sports sections of newspapers are locally and regionally oriented. The *Dallas Morning News* in its sports coverage focuses almost all its attention on the Southwest Conference and other Texas schools. The *Lexington Herald-Leader* covers the University of Kentucky and the Southeastern Conference. This regional orientation will tend to steer coverage toward problems at the institutional or conference level. Payments to players, the hiring and firing of

---

column a much publicized chair-throwing incident by Knight at a game. A reader charged that the column "read like a legal brief prepared on behalf of the defendant." The writer's response to Feinstein: "Probably, he was right."

coaches, the impact of Proposition 48 on a particular school, and the like become the areas of local interest. Less attention is concentrated on the NCAA as a whole. However, it is precisely this perspective that is needed to understand the cartel aspects of college athletics.

One other factor which may play a role in the absence of cartel stories is the long-run dynamics of sports journalism. Prior to the 1970s, sports coverage tended to report on-the-field action and leave investigative reporting and editorializing to the "hard news" departments. Since the 1970s, however, investigative reporting within the sports section has grown considerably. Most likely, at one time the local newspapers would have been very slow to move on the SMU and University of Kentucky stories. This explanation suggests that, as sports journalism continues to develop, coverage of the cartel aspects of the NCAA will become more likely.

With these three speculative explanations in hand, there is still a paradox with respect to the media. No one explanation provides a completely satisfactory answer. The media investigate some sports stories without regard to access. In addition, some of the sports media, such as *Sports Illustrated* and the *National*, are investigative and have a national rather than a regional perspective and audience. Yet the NCAA as a cartel does not receive any press or air time. Without a theory of media behavior, we simply must conclude that the answer to the media's paradoxical behavior in the case of the NCAA lies elsewhere.

Players

Occasionally, a college athlete generates a little noise about problems in college athletics, but for the most part athletes are a silent voice. For instance, two athletes at the urging of the AAU challenged the NCAA's eligibility rules in 1970. Given the substantial transfer of rents away from athletes toward other actors in the NCAA, this relative silence presents a curiosity. Why have athletes not led a reform movement if indeed rents are being taken from them? Although they are only eighteen to twenty-two years old, individuals of similar ages are often outspoken with regard to topics such as war and voting. Additionally, while they may have inelastic supply curves, college athletes have market alternatives. What explains their passive role?[8]

To present an effective response to a well-organized and financed monopsony, athletes would need to organize. However, such organization of a labor movement takes time. Students are in college for only four or five years, usually not enough time to become disgruntled and active about NCAA policy. Related to this, there is a public goods problem. If it takes an enormous amount of time to get reforms passed in the NCAA, an individual athlete has no incentive to lobby for reform. He will bear all of the costs of lobbying but will receive none of the benefits, since he will already have graduated or used up his eligibility. Moreover, as in the case of professional sports, the antitrust protection extended to college athletes is uncertain. The link between academics and sports along with the educational rhetoric of the NCAA places college athletes in a different position from most workers, even though the NCAA is a $1 billion per year industry. Workers in other non-sports industries could easily present and win cases with the type of explicit restraints on wages that exist within the NCAA. College athletes, in contrast, do not have this certainty.

In spite of these roadblocks, college athletes seem to be slowly moving toward more organization. In the last few years, disgruntled basketball players have threatened to quit or actually refused to play for coaches at two major universities. In both cases, coaching changes occurred after the season ended. When Clemson's successful football coach, Dan Ford, was forced to resign because of an NCAA investigation, the players threatened but did not follow through on a mass walk-

8. For a look at the pros and cons of organization by athletes, see *Sports, Inc.*, January 9, 1989, pp. 24–25. Obviously, a conflict arises, as the article points out, when the Rose Bowl generates $17 million and the producers of the affair (student athletes) receive nothing. A telling point is made by the athletic director at the University of Pittsburgh, Ed Bozik. "It's just inconsistent with the purposes and the goals of the University. If we are doing our business properly, educating students, we are not paying them for their services." Professors, faculty, staff, and some students, such as newspaper workers, are paid for their services. Why not athletes?

out. Whether one views such actions as the result of undisciplined and spoiled players or as labor revolts, these actions signal an evolving problem for the NCAA cartel.

Legal System

Legislatures and courts have undertaken some review and reform of policies in college athletics. Yet many of the legislative reforms have resulted in giving the NCAA's collusive restraints the force of law. Much of the recent interest in college athletics by the legal system has originated at the state level. Courts, by their nature, have taken a more passive role because they must wait for cases to come before them.

State legislatures have taken the lead in reforms surrounding college athletics. Most of this interest centers away from cartel questions. Agent-athlete relationships have garnered the largest share of attention. Several states have passed laws requiring registration by sports agents and imposing penalties on agents who provide financial benefits to athletes with college eligibility remaining.[9] This is a key example where the effect of reform is to make some of the NCAA eligibility rules carry the force of law. A few legislatures have even considered making any payment to athletes not sanctioned by the NCAA a criminal offense. On the other side, the Nevada state legislature (in view of the Jerry Tarkanian case) has passed a bill which puts a limit on some of the NCAA's cartel powers. Essentially, the bill requires any penalties imposed upon a Nevada state institution to have followed standard due process. Such legislation has also been considered in Nebraska, Illinois, and Florida. In a slightly different vein, legislators in Nebraska and Illinois have also offered bills which would allow payments to student athletes. Some legislators have even proposed entrenching conference power. In Texas, some state legislators threatened to cut off funding to the University of Texas and Texas A&M if they exited the Southwest Conference.

Again, though, the net result of much of the legislation has strengthened the NCAA's cartel powers. As an example, in

9. As of October 1, 1989 well over fifty pieces of legislation were pending in state legislatures related to college athletics. The legislation encompassed such subjects as athletic agents, anabolic steroids, liability, and ticket scalping (*NCAA News*, October 9, 1989, p. 10).

1954 Congress exempted college athletics from the federal admissions tax (Falla 1981, p. 207), thus granting college athletics a competitive advantage over alternative forms of entertainment. In 1961 Congress prohibited professional football from telecasting from stations within seventy-five miles of an intercollegiate game (Falla 1981, pp. 183, 243). This also reduced the range of substitutes for the entertainment provided by college athletics. Over this century Congress has occasionally turned its attention to college sports. In more recent times, most of its attention has centered upon hearings rather than contemplating new legislation, but lately this situation has changed. In the late 1970s the House of Representatives conducted hearings into the investigative and enforcement procedures of the NCAA. A representative from Nevada, upset by the NCAA's handling of Jerry Tarkanian of the UNLV, provided the impetus for the hearings. No legislation came out of these hearings, although the majority of the House subcommittee issued many strong criticisms of the NCAA enforcement process. More recently, two former college athletes, Representative Tom McMillan and Senator Bill Bradley, and others have expressed an interest in requiring disclosure of the graduation rates of athletes playing at NCAA member schools and in denying federal funds for noncompliance.[10] At the time of this writing, the legislation is still pending. Such a requirement is a first step, at the federal level, toward making eligibility requirements carry the force of law.

The courts, although recipients of actions initiated by others, have also played a role in reform. They have taken part in the agent-player reforms. Some of the recent cases in federal court have involved charges of fraud and racketeering. Also, the federal courts have taken the most interest in the cartel aspects of the NCAA. Most notable is the findings of the Supreme Court in the Oklahoma-Georgia case, to which we have referred many times. In that case the Court found the NCAA television plan to be a collusive restraint in violation of the Sherman Act. This decision addressed the NCAA's monopoly power but left its monopsony power over athletes intact. Questions of law peripheral to the NCAA, such as drug enforcement

10. See *Washington Post*, September 13, 1989, section G.

and due process, have received some attention in the courts. But as noted above, the courts are a passive agent in the reform process. Some other agent must take the step of putting NCAA issues before a court.

2. The 1991 NCAA Convention

It was widely anticipated that the 1991 NCAA convention would enact landmark reforms in college athletics. It was thought that university presidents and academic administrators would take control of the destiny of college athletics away from coaches and athletic directors. What actually happened is summarized as follows.

With respect to program "costs," the following measures passed by vote of the members: scholarship reductions of 10 percent (from ninety-five to eighty-five in Division I-A football by 1994–95 and fifteen to thirteen in basketball by 1993–94); coaching staff reductions (from sixteen to thirteen in football and from five to four in basketball); reductions in paid visits by recruits and off-campus visits by coaches; restrictions on away-game departure and return times; increases per school in minimum sport participation (from six to seven for both men's and women's sports); and a minimum financial aid standard outside of football and basketball of $250,000 (including academic aid). The following resolutions which directly affect players, some of which also relate to "costs," passed: a restriction on maximum practice time per day (four hours) and per week (twenty hours over six days); slight reductions in season length other than in football (from twenty-eight to twenty-seven basketball games); prohibition of summer scholarships for incoming freshmen; provision for U.S. Olympic Committee coverage of athletic training expenses; a phase-out of athletic dormitories by 1996; reduction of training table meals to one per day by 1996; and consideration of athlete eligibility for a professional draft without loss of collegiate eligibility. Other measures which passed included a measure allowing Division I-A football schools to set their own financial aid standards by 1993; future consideration of a low-budget Division I-AAA football category; and elimination of the bowl signing date (the bowl organizations had already limited themselves with a provision for financial penalties).

Other proposals were either rejected or never brought up for a vote. The membership rejected a requirement of a 50 percent graduation rate and a minimum grade point average rule, but adopted a provision that athletes must have completed 50 percent of the requirements for a degree before their fourth year of eligibility. Also, the members defeated an amendment to Proposition 48 that would have granted an additional year of eligibility to initial nonqualifiers who made satisfactory progress once in college. Also, though some hinted at the possibility, no due process provisions were added to the NCAA enforcement process.

From the analytical viewpoint of this book, the 1991 convention produced superficial rather than substantive changes. Many of the reforms are so slight as not to constrain behavior (for example, the move from twenty-eight to twenty-seven basketball games). The practice time limits remain at a level that is high in practical terms—four hours can be spent five days a week or three hours six days a week. In addition, the lead time on the cuts in staff and scholarships leaves room for later amendment, which is not uncommon.[11] Also, the rejection of graduation rate provisions and the lack of consideration of due process issues are instructive in their own right. Overall, the "reform convention" was more akin to adding new tail fins to the same old vehicle.

Moreover, the impetus for whatever reforms occurred during the convention provides even stronger support for the analysis in this book of NCAA-initiated reforms. Much of the true initiation of reform or the appearance of it owes to outside pressures. The enactment of more institutional-level control, higher academic standards, and time limitations on practices in each case was motivated by congressional pressure. As the outgoing NCAA president described it, "Like it or lament it, the sabre-rattling of this kind has an effect."[12] The NCAA executive director warned that, "if the NCAA doesn't take steps to pass these reform issues, there's good support for congres-

11. As Mike Krzyzewski, head basketball coach at Duke and chairman of the National Association of Basketball Coaches, put it, "If it says August 1992 (as is the case with staff cuts), we have an opportunity to refine the total package. The administrators will listen." See *USA Today*, January 9, 1991, p. 4C.

12. NCAA president Al Witte in *USA Today*, January 7, 1991, p. 2C.

sional action."[13] Moreover, moves by several state legislatures prompted the talk of enforcement process revision although it has not yet yielded any changes.

In addition to the reform talk generated by exogenous forces, many of the so-called reforms represent a continuation of the same old intra-NCAA struggles for the rewards of cartelization. The more stringent Division I eligibility requirements are a clear-cut example. As the North Carolina A&T president said, "The haves want to divide a greater amount of revenue among . . . fewer . . . people."[14] While the more stringent eligibility requirements show how the big-time football producers can squeeze the other schools, the same incentives can work the other way. To a large extent, the scholarship cuts and athletic dormitory and training table provisions are an attempt by smaller schools to limit the talent pool and long-cherished physical capital advantages of the larger schools. Several football coaches, including Joe Paterno (Penn State), Tom Osborne (Nebraska), and George Perles (Michigan State), spoke out against the coaching staff cuts. On the dormitory and training table issue, the athletic director of Tennessee said, "Some people have no business voting on what I'm doing, and I've got no business voting on what they are doing."[15] Even the supposed cost containment provision of scholarship cuts can be viewed as mainly an intraschool redistribution. Where athletic departments pay universities actual dollars (usually from athletic foundations) for grant-in-aids to student athletes at average costs but the marginal costs are very low, the scholarship cuts simply reduce the dollars in the hands of athletic departments at the expense of the general fund.

3. The Knight Commission Report

In March 1990, a commission of twenty-two members sponsored by the Knight Foundation issued its report on the reform

13. NCAA executive director Dick Schultz in *USA Today,* January 7, 1991, p. 2C.

14. *USA Today,* January 9, 1991, p. 4C. Canisius's president said, "This is an issue which could stretch the viability of the NCAA . . . if we are going to be at the mercy of multi-million dollar football programs, then the NCAA is not the organization for a school like ours." Terry Holland, athletic director at Davidson, said the NCAA "talked about cost containment, and now we're being asked to spend more."

15. See *USA Today,* January 9, 1991, p. 4C.

of intercollegiate athletics.[16] Although the report has the appearance of an external study of the NCAA, it actually represents another attempt at reform from within the organization. Out of the twenty-two commission members, sixteen were present or former executive officers or board members of universities. The co-chairmen were former presidents at Notre Dame University and of the State University System of North Carolina. In addition, the executive director of the NCAA served on the commission.

The report made several recommendations for college athletics. Among these were that college presidents assume responsibility for and control of policies, personnel, and finances; that all athletic revenues be channeled through general treasury accounts; that athletes make adequate progress toward their degrees; that annual audits of the academic and financial positions of athletes and programs be undertaken; that the graduation rates and college experiences of athletes be similar to those of the general student population; and that athletics be operated within the general mission of the university. The report called for an initial movement toward reform in four primary areas: first and foremost, presidential control, followed by academic integrity, fiscal management, and independent certification.

This most recent reform study shares most of the characteristics of other internal reform efforts within the NCAA. First, the recommendations serve as much as a marketing tool as they do as substantive reform proposals. The issue of presidential control and responsibility stands at the leading edge of the report. Yet, as has been discussed previously, the perception that coaches and athletic directors have dominated NCAA and institutional decisions in the past is overplayed. University executives do not currently and have not generally removed themselves from control of athletic programs. Membership composition on the NCAA Council as well as experience on college campuses refutes the notion that athletic executives and college presidents do not at present exert their influence. Second, to whatever extent actual reform is intended, the rec-

16. Because the authors did not possess a copy of the Knight report at the time of this writing, their information about its content relies on articles from the *New York Times*, March 20, 1991, p. D25, and *USA Today*, March 20, 1991, p. c5. The analysis of the Knight Commission's report is therefore necessarily scanty.

ommendations of the Knight Commission fall into the category of reallocating the rewards among cartel members rather than altering the power of the cartel itself. For instance, the report stresses the importance of placing athletic revenues of any kind within the general university treasury. This would not reduce cartel returns; it would simply increase the discretion of university executives over those returns. Likewise, the insistence that certain academic standards be upheld would have the impact discussed in previous chapters of shifting the competitive balance between some schools and conferences. Thus, whatever comes of the Knight Commission's report, the overall cartel power of the NCAA would be unchanged.

At bottom, the major problem posed by the NCAA as a cartel is that student athletes are economically exploited by the monopsony power of the system. All the other aspects of the NCAA's behavior relate in some way to this fundamental issue. The recommendations of the 1991 NCAA convention and the Knight Commission in no way whatsoever resolve the issue of compensating athletes for their services. Until this is done, the rest of the so-called reform movement can be seen for what it is: a bunch of people shedding crocodile tears for the young men and women on the playing field.

4. Concluding Remarks

Reforms have occurred within college athletics. Most of these reforms have originated within the NCAA to strengthen its monopsony position or as a struggle over the distribution of cartel rents. To the extent that reforms have originated outside the NCAA, many of them have worked in conjunction with NCAA rules to strengthen its cartel power.

Whether or not the cartel aspects of the NCAA will come under scrutiny in the near future is difficult to predict. College athletics are tremendously popular, and the demand for them grows yearly. Most would-be reformers are probably hesitant to tamper with such success. On the other hand, the Olympic movement and USOC grappled with some of the same problems in the 1970s and overcame many of them to the satisfaction of most parties, including athletes. Before the 1980s, amateur athletes in most Olympic sports were barred from receiving direct, pecuniary reimbursement. Secret payments to athletes became common, and U.S. athletes were at a disadvantage because of the subsidization of athletes in many other countries. In response, a new system of amateur athletics emerged which maintained the desirable, competitive aspects of the sports but allowed for compensation of athletes.

The NCAA continues to face the problem that ultimately sounds the death knell for most cartels, that is, the instability created by intracartel factions. Any dissolution of the monopsony power of the NCAA may ultimately owe less to outside reform than it does to the difficulty of maintaining collusive agreements between heterogeneous producers. The controversy and ill will created by the Notre Dame network television package illustrate the tenuous position in which most cartels eventually find themselves. Additionally, with the large and increasing revenues involved and the restraints on labor compensation, it is not likely that the NCAA's rhetoric and stopgap measures will end the secret flow of dollars to athletes. In contrast, this cartel destabilizing force will most likely continue to amaze onlookers of college sports.

Appendixes

APPENDIX ONE

Winning Percentage and Its Variability by School, 1953–83

Team	Winning Percentage*	Standard Deviation	Coefficient of Variation
Air Force	.403	.261	.647
Alabama	.746	.250	.335
Arizona	.525	.187	.356
Arizona State	.745	.169	.227
Arkansas	.693	.178	.257
Army	.504	.256	.508
Auburn	.677	.187	.276
Baylor	.464	.222	.478
Boston College	.598	.182	.304
Brigham Young	.511	.260	.509
California	.416	.187	.449
Cincinnati	.484	.201	.415
Clemson	.589	.201	.341
Colorado	.548	.224	.409
Colorado State	.389	.210	.540
Duke	.510	.173	.339
East Carolina	.600	.218	.363
Florida	.612	.174	.284
Florida State	.566	.213	.376
Georgia	.636	.223	.351
Georgia Tech	.560	.203	.363
Houston	.601	.197	.328
Illinois	.470	.252	.536
Indiana	.343	.184	.536
Iowa	.451	.250	.554

Team	Winning Percentage*	Standard Deviation	Coefficient of Variation
Iowa State	.430	.176	.409
Kansas	.422	.207	.490
Kansas State	.309	.189	.612
Kentucky	.430	.202	.470
Louisiana State	.648	.191	.295
Louisville	.514	.210	.409
Maryland	.538	.234	.435
Memphis State	.558	.216	.387
Miami (FL)	.539	.203	.377
Michigan	.694	.200	.288
Michigan State	.576	.219	.380
Minnesota	.493	.202	.410
Mississippi	.664	.217	.327
Mississippi State	.446	.231	.525
Missouri	.598	.190	.318
Navy	.537	.223	.415
Nebraska	.688	.235	.342
New Mexico	.479	.211	.441
New Mexico State	.438	.218	.498
North Carolina	.533	.217	.407
North Carolina State	.493	.222	.450
Northwestern	.314	.216	.688
Notre Dame	.701	.223	.318
Ohio State	.781	.162	.207
Oklahoma	.782	.188	.240
Oklahoma State	.468	.164	.350
Oregon	.447	.195	.436
Oregon State	.455	.250	.549
Penn State	.758	.138	.182
Pittsburgh	.541	.261	.482
Purdue	.580	.187	.322
Rice	.359	.226	.629
Rutgers	.587	.208	.354
South Carolina	.486	.157	.323
Southern California	.717	.214	.303
Southern Methodist	.479	.227	.474
Southern Mississippi	.533	.208	.390
Stanford	.505	.188	.372
Syracuse	.562	.201	.358
Temple	.475	.246	.518
Tennessee	.642	.163	.254
Texas	.746	.192	.257
Texas A&M	.468	.231	.494

Team	Winning Percentage*	Standard Deviation	Coefficient of Variation
Texas Christian	.367	.225	.613
Texas–El Paso	.361	.259	.717
Texas Tech	.516	.229	.443
Tulane	.368	.193	.524
Tulsa	.524	.226	.431
UCLA	.662	.212	.320
Utah	.490	.197	.402
Utah State	.572	.187	.327
Vanderbilt	.359	.206	.574
Virginia	.306	.181	.592
Virginia Tech	.580	.182	.314
Wake Forest	.306	.178	.582
Washington	.568	.216	.380
Washington State	.393	.181	.461
West Virginia	.581	.214	.368
Wisconsin	.466	.216	.464
Wyoming	.582	.227	.390

*Winning percentage is computed by dividing total wins by total wins plus losses; ties are ignored. The winning percentages and standard deviations for Southern Mississippi are at the mean of the other schools.

A P P E N D I X T W O

Number of Top Twenty
Finishes, 1953–83

School	Times in Top Twenty	School	Times in Top Twenty
Ohio State	26	Maryland	8
Oklahoma*	25	Miami (FL)*	8
Southern California*	25	West Virginia	8
Alabama	23	Army	7
Texas	21	Iowa	7
Penn State	20	North Carolina	7
Notre Dame	20	Southern Methodist*	7
Michigan	18	Stanford	7
Auburn*	18	Texas A&M*	7
Nebraska	17	Baylor	6
UCLA	16	Duke	6
Arkansas	16	Florida State	6
Louisiana State	15	Minnesota*	6
Mississippi	14	Mississippi State*	6
Georgia	13	Navy	6
Pittsburgh	12	North Carolina State	6
Tennessee	12	Oregon State	6
Arizona State*	11	Wisconsin	6
Michigan State*	11	Brigham Young	5
Washington	11	Illinois*	5
Georgia Tech	10	Rice	5
Houston*	10	Air Force	4
Missouri	10	Texas Christian	4
Purdue	10	Texas Tech	4
Syracuse	10	Kentucky*	3
Florida*	9	Kansas*	3
Clemson*	8	Rutgers	3
Colorado*	8	Wyoming*	3

School	Times in Top Twenty	School	Times in Top Twenty
Arizona*	2	Texas–El Paso	1
California*	2	Tulsa*	1
Indiana	2	Utah State	1
Oklahoma State*	2	Utah	1
Tulane	2	Washington State	1
Virginia Tech	2	Colorado State	0
Boston College	1	Cincinnati	0
East Carolina	1	Kansas State*	0
Iowa State*	1	New Mexico	0
Louisville	1	Southern Mississippi*	0
Memphis State	1	Temple	0
New Mexico State	1	Vanderbilt	0
Northwestern	1	Virginia	0
Oregon*	1	Wake Forest	0
South Carolina*	1		

*Designates NCAA probation.

APPENDIX THREE

School and Conference SAT (ACT) Scores, 1986

School	SAT	SAT (Conf)	School	SAT	SAT (Conf)
Alabama	982	999	Louisville	792	1051
Arizona	984	1058	Maryland	1025	1125
Arizona St.	967	1058	Memphis St.*	906	1051
Arkansas*	924	1026	Michigan	1180	1061
Army	1175	1051	Michigan St.	1006	1061
Auburn	1072	999	Minnesota*	976	1061
Baylor	1037	1026	Mississippi*	941	999
Boston College	1104	1051	Mississippi St.*	985	999
Brigham Young*	1034	938	Missouri	1012	964
California	1181	1058	Navy	1241	1241
Cincinnati	999	1051	Nebraska*	928	964
Clemson	1027	1125	New Mexico	792	938
Colorado	1066	964	New Mexico St.	805	—
Colorado St.	984	938	North Carolina	1087	1125
Duke	1295	1125	North Carolina St.	1023	1125
Florida	1109	999	Northwestern	1220	1061
Florida St.	1017	1051	Notre Dame	1210	1051
Georgia	1016	999	Ohio St.	993	1061
Georgia Tech	1186	1125	Oklahoma*	924	964
Houston	986	1026	Oklahoma St.*	915	964
Illinois	1116	1061	Oregon	972	1058
Indiana	991	1061	Oregon St.	951	1058
Iowa*	1056	1056	Penn State	1093	1051
Iowa St.*	980	964	Pittsburgh	1012	1051
Kansas*	959	964	Purdue	1007	1061
Kansas St.*	928	964	Rice	1321	1026
Kentucky*	954	954	Rutgers	1071	1051
Louisiana St.	871	999	South Carolina	957	1051

School	SAT	SAT (Conf)	School	SAT	SAT (Conf)
Southern California	1017	1058	UCLA	1087	1058
SMU	1094	1026	Utah*	915	938
Stanford	1290	1058	Utah St.	853	—
Syracuse	1140	1051	Vanderbilt	1177	999
Temple	984	1051	Virginia	1223	1125
Tennessee*	884	999	Virginia Tech	1103	1051
Texas	1067	1626	Wake Forest	1139	1125
Texas A&M	924	1026	Washington	1078	1058
Texas Christian	—	—	Washington St.	—	—
Texas–El Paso	—	—	West Virginia	902	1051
Texas Tech*	860	1026	Wisconsin	1080	1061
Tulane	1136	1051	Wyoming	968	938
Tulsa	1086	1051			

Note: Independents are treated as a single conference.
Source: American Colleges and Universities (1983).
*ACT score multiplied by 44.

APPENDIX FOUR
Membership on NCAA Council by Year

1952   Alabama, Brown, Colorado College, Drake, University of Michigan, Oberlin, Pittsburgh, Santa Clara, Southern Methodist University, Stanford, Texas A&M, Tulsa, Utah State, and Virginia Tech.

1953   Brown, Drake, Franklin and Marshall, University of Michigan, Oberlin, Pittsburgh, Santa Clara, University of South California, Southern Methodist University, Texas A&M, Tulsa, Utah State, Virginia Tech, and University of Washington.

1954   Brown, Citadel, Dartmouth, Drake, Franklin and Marshall, University of Michigan, Oberlin, Pittsburgh, Santa Clara, Southern Methodist University, Texas Christian, Tufts, Tulsa, Utah State, Vanderbilt, and University of Washington.

1955   Brown, Citadel, University of Colorado, Drake, Franklin and Marshall, Harvard, University of Iowa, Lehigh, Oberlin, Santa Clara, Southern Methodist University, Texas Christian, Utah State, Vanderbilt, and University of Washington.

1956   Beloit College, Brown, University of California at Santa Barbara, Citadel, University of Colorado, Drake, Harvard, Lehigh, University of North Carolina at Chapel Hill, Rutgers, Southern Methodist University, Texas Christian, and University of Washington.

1957   Beloit College, Brown, University of California at Santa Barbara, Citadel, University of Colorado, University of Denver, Houston, Lehigh, University of North Carolina at Chapel Hill, Rutgers, Stanford, Texas Christian, and Yale.

1958   Beloit College, University of California at Santa Barbara, Citadel, University of Colorado, University of Denver, Houston, Lehigh, University of Massachusetts at Amherst, University of Michigan, University of North Carolina at Chapel Hill, University of Pennsylvania, San Jose State University, Stanford, Texas Christian, and Yale.

1959   University of Arkansas at Fayetteville, University of California at Santa Barbara, Citadel, Colgate, University of Colorado, Dartmouth, University of Iowa, University of Massachusetts at Amherst, University of Michigan, Montana State, University of North Carolina at Chapel Hill, University of Pennsylvania, San Jose State University, Stanford, University of Texas at El Paso, and Wichita State.

1960   University of Arkansas at Fayetteville, University of California at Santa Barbara, Colgate, University of Colorado, Dartmouth, Davidson College, DePauw, University of Iowa, University of Massachusetts at Amherst, Montana State, University of North Carolina at Chapel Hill, Pennsylvania State University, Stanford, University of Texas at El Paso, Wichita State, and University of Wisconsin at Madison.

1961   University of Arkansas at Fayetteville, Colgate, Dartmouth, Davidson College, DePauw, University of Iowa, University of Massachusetts at Amherst, Montana State, University of North Carolina at Chapel Hill, University of Oklahoma, Oregon State, Pennsylvania State, South Dakota State, Wichita State, and Williams College.

1962   University of Arkansas at Fayetteville, Brigham Young University, University of Chicago, Colgate, Colorado State, Davidson College, DePauw, University of Georgia, University of Iowa, University of Oklahoma, Oregon State, Pennsylvania State University, South Dakota State, University of Texas at Austin, Wichita State, and Williams College,

1963   Brigham Young University, University of Chicago, Colorado State, University of Georgia, University of Michigan, University of Oklahoma, Oregon State, Pennsylvania State University, University of the South, South Dakota State, Swarthmore, University of Texas at Austin, Texas A&M, Wichita State, and Williams College.

1964   Brigham Young University, University of Chicago, Colorado State, Hampton Institute, Knox College, University of Michigan, University of Oklahoma, Oregon State, Pennsylvania State University, University of the South, Swarthmore, University of Tennessee at Knoxville, Texas A&M, Wichita State, and Williams College.

1965   University of Arizona, University of California at Los Angeles, Colorado State, Hampton Institute, Knox College, University of Michigan, University of Missouri at Columbia, Oregon State, Pennsylvania State University, University of the

South, Swarthmore, University of Tennessee at Knoxville, Texas A&M, Wheaton College, and Williams College.

1966 University of Arizona, Brigham Young University, University of California at Los Angeles, Colorado State University, Hampton Institute, Howard, Knox College, University of Michigan, University of Missouri at Columbia, Oregon State, Pennsylvania State University, University of Tennessee at Knoxville, Texas A&M, Tufts, and Wheaton College.

1967 University of Arizona, Brigham Young University, University of California at Los Angeles, Colorado State, Howard, Johns Hopkins University, Knox College, University of Missouri at Columbia, Ohio State, Oregon State, University of Pittsburgh, University of Tennessee at Knoxville, Texas Tech, Tufts, and Wheaton College.

1968 Brigham Young University, University of California at Los Angeles, Colorado State, University of Georgia, Howard, Johns Hopkins University, University of Missouri at Columbia, Ohio State, University of Oklahoma, University of Pittsburgh, University of Tennessee at Knoxville, Texas Tech, Tufts, and Union College.

1969 Brigham Young University, University of Georgia, Howard, Johns Hopkins University, Lincoln University (Missouri), University of Missouri at Columbia, Ohio State, University of Oklahoma, University of Oregon, University of Pittsburgh, University of Tennessee at Knoxville, Texas Tech, Union College, and Valparaiso.

1970 University of Arizona, University of California at Berkeley, University of Georgia, Howard, Lincoln University (Missouri), University of Missouri at Columbia, Ohio State, University of Oklahoma, University of Oregon, University of Pittsburgh, University of Tennessee at Knoxville, Texas Tech, Union College, Valparaiso, and Worcester Polytechnic Institute.

1971 University of Arizona, California State University at Fresno, University of Georgia, Michigan State, University of Oklahoma, University of Pittsburgh, Temple University, Tennessee State, Texas Tech, Union College, Valparaiso, University of Washington, and Worcester Polytechnic Institute.

1972 University of Arizona, University of Chicago, California State University at Fresno, University of Kansas, Kent State, Michigan State, North Carolina State, University of Oklahoma, Temple University, Tennessee State, Texas Tech, Valapraiso, University of Washington, and Worcester Polytechnic Institute.

1973   University of Arizona, California State University at Fresno, University of Indiana, Kent State, Massachusetts Institute of Technology, Michigan State, North Carolina State, University of Oklahoma, South Dakota State, Temple University, Tennessee State, University of Texas at Austin, Texas Tech, University of Washington, and Worcester Polytechnic Institute.

1974   University of Chicago, Colorado State, California State University at Fresno, Fort Valley College, University of Indiana, Kent State, University of Maine at Orono, Massachusetts Institute of Technology, Michigan State, Mulenberg College, North Carolina State, South Dakota State, Temple University, and University of Texas at Austin.

1975   University of California at Davis, Colorado State, East Stroudsburg State, Fort Valley College, University of Indiana, Lincoln University (Missouri), University of Maine at Orono, Massachusetts Institute of Technology, Mulenberg College, North Carolina State, Ohio Wesleyan, University of the Pacific, Temple University, University of Texas at Austin, and University of Toledo.

1976   University of Alabama, University of California at Davis, Colorado State, East Stroudsburg State, Fort Valley College, University of Illinois at Champaign, Lincoln University (Missouri), University of Maine at Orono, Massachusetts Institute of Technology, Mulenberg College, Ohio Wesleyan, University of the Pacific, Temple University, University of Texas at Austin, and University of Toledo.

1977   University of Alabama, University of California at Davis, Colorado State, University of Connecticut, East Stroudsburg State, Fisk College, University of Illinois at Champaign, Lincoln University (Missouri), Massachusetts Institute of Technology, Ohio University, Ohio Wesleyan, University of the Pacific, South Dakota State, Temple University, and Texas Christian.

BIBLIOGRAPHY

Alchian, Armen A., and Allen, William R. 1969. *Exchange and Production Theory in Use.* Belmont, CA: Wadsworth Publishing.

Alchian, Armen A., and Demsetz, Harold. 1972. "Production, Information Costs and Economic Organization." *American Economic Review* 62 (December): 775–95.

American Council on Education. 1983. *American Universities and Colleges.* New York: Walter de Gruyter.

Asch, Peter, and Seneca, Joseph J. 1975. "Characteristics of Collusive Firms." *Journal of Industrial Economics* 23 (March): 223–37.

Baker, W. J. 1982. *Sports in the Western World.* Totowa, NJ.

Becker, Gary. 1983. "A Theory of Competition among Pressure Groups for Political Influence." *Quarterly Journal of Economics* 98 (August): 371–400.

_____ . 1985. "College Athletes Should Get Paid What They Are Worth." *Business Week*, September 30, p. 18.

_____ . 1987. "The NCAA: A Cartel in Sheepskin Clothing." *Business Week*, September 14, p. 24.

Board of Regents of the University of Oklahoma et al. v. the National Collegiate Athletic Association. 1982. 546 F. Supp. 1276 (WD OK).

Boreland, Melvin V., Goff, Brian L, and Pulsinelli, Robert W. 1989. "College Athletics: Financial Burden or Boom?" Bowling Green: Western Kentucky University.

Browning, Edgar K., and Browning, Jaqueline M. 1989. *Microeconomic Theory and Applications.* Glenview, IL: Scott, Foresman & Co.

Buchanan, James M., Tollison, Robert D., and Tullock, Gordon. 1980. *Toward a Theory of the Rent-Seeking Society.* College Station: Texas A&M University Press.

Buchanan, James M., and Tullock, Gordon. 1962. *The Calculus of Consent.* Ann Arbor: University of Michigan Press.

Cairns, J., Jennet, N., and Sloane, P. J. 1986. "The Economics of Professional Team Sports: A Survey of Theory and Evidence." *Journal of Economic Studies* 13:1–80.

Carlton, Dennis, and Perloff, Jeffrey. 1990. *Modern Industrial Organization.* Glenview, IL: Scott, Foresman & Co.

Chu, Donald, Segrave, Jeffrey, and Becker, Beverly, eds. 1985. *Sports and Higher Education.* Champaign, IL: Human Kinetics Publishers.

Coughlin, Cletus C., and Erekson, Homer O. 1984. "An Examination of Contributions to Support Intercollegiate Athletics." *Southern Economic Journal* 51 (July): 180–95.

Eckert, Ross D. 1981. "The Life Cycle of Regulatory Commissioners." *Journal of Law and Economics* 24 (April): 113–20.

Falla, Jack. 1981. *NCAA: The Voice of College Sports.* Mission, KS: National Collegiate Athletic Association.

Feinstein, John. 1986. *A Season on the Brink.* New York: Macmillan.

——— . 1988. *A Season Inside.* New York: Villard Books.

Flath, Arnold W. 1963. "The History of the Relations between the National Collegiate Athletic Association and the Amateur Athletic Union in the United States." Ph.D. dissertation, University of Michigan.

Fleisher, A. A., Goff, B. L., Shughart. W. F., and Tollison, R. D. 1988. "Crime or Punishment? Enforcement of the NCAA Football Cartel." *Journal of Economic Behavior and Organization* 10:433–51.

Frey, James H. 1982. *The Governance of Collegiate Athletics.* West Point, NY: Leisure Press.

Goff, Brian, Shughart, William F., and Tollison, R. D. 1988. "Disqualification by Decree: Amateur Rules as Barriers to Entry." *Journal of Institutional and Theoretical Economics* 144 (June): 515–23.

Green, Edward, and Porter, Robert. 1984. "Noncooperative Collusion under Imperfect Price Competition." *Econometrica* 52 (January): 87–100.

Greenspan, David. 1988. "College Football's Biggest Fumble: The Economic Impact of the Supreme Court's Decision in *National Collegiate Athletic Association vs. Board of Regents of the University of Oklahoma.*" *Antitrust Bulletin* 33, no. 1: 1–65.

Hart-Nibring, Nand, and Cottingham, Clement. 1986. *The Political Economy of College Sports.* Lexington, MA: Lexington Books.

Ivey, Mark, and Rubinstein, Sharon. 1986. "How Educators Are Fighting Big-Money Madness in Athletics." *Business Week,* October 27, p. 136.

Jenkins, Dan. 1966. "It's One Point Six Pick Up Sticks." *Sports Illustrated,* March 21, pp. 30–31.

——— . 1967. "The Fighting Illini." *Sports Illustrated,* March 6, pp. 16–19.

Koch, James V. 1973. "A Troubled Cartel: The NCAA." *Law and Contemporary Problems* 38 (Winter/Spring), pgs. 39–69.

_____ . 1983. "Intercollegiate Athletics: An Economic Explanation." *Social Science Quarterly* 64, no. 2: 360–374.

Koch, James V., and Wilbert, M. Leonard. 1978. "The NCAA: A Socioeconomic Analysis." *American Journal of Economics and Sociology* 37, no. 3 (July): 225–39.

Lawrence, Paul R. 1982. "The Intercollegiate Athletic Cartel: The Economics, History and Legal Arrangements of the National Collegiate Athletic Association." Ph.D. dissertation, Virginia Polytechnic Institute and State University.

_____ . 1987. *Unsportsmanlike Conduct: The National Collegiate Athletic Association and the Business of College Sports.* New York: Praeger Publishers.

Lehman, Andrea, ed. 1988. *Peterson's Annual Guide to Undergraduate Study: Guide to Four-Year Colleges, 1988.* Princeton, NJ: Peterson's Guide.

Lewis, Guy M. 1969. "Theodore Roosevelt's Role in the 1905 Football Controversy." *Research Quarterly* 40, no. 4 (December): 717–24.

McCallum, John D., and Pearson, Charles. 1972. *College Football U.S.A., 1869–1971.* New York: McGraw-Hill.

McCormick, Robert E., and Meiners, Roger. 1987. "Bust the College Sports Cartel." *Fortune,* October 12, pp. 235–36.

McCormick, Robert E., and Tinsley, Maurice. 1987. "Athletic versus Academics? Evidence from SAT Scores." *Journal of Political Economy* 95:1103–16.

_____ . Forthcoming. "Athletics and Academics: A Model of University Contributions." In B. L. Goff and R. D. Tollison, eds., *Sportometrics.* College Station: Texas A&M University Press.

McCormick, Robert E., and Tollison, Robert D. 1981. *Politicians, Legislation, and the Economy: An Inquiry into the Interest Group Theory of Government.* Boston: Martinus-Nijhoff.

McGee, John. 1988. *Industrial Organization.* Englewood Cliffs, NJ: Prentice-Hall.

McKenzie, Richard B., and Sullivan, Thomas E. 1985. "Does the NCAA Exploit College Athletes? An Economic and Legal Reinterpretation." *Antitrust Bulletin* 33 (Summer): 373–99.

National Center for Education Statistics. 1983. *Digest of Education Statistics, 1982.* Washington D.C.: U.S. Government Printing Office.

National Collegiate Athletic Association. 1985. *1984 NCAA Football Television Committee Report.* Mission, KS: National Collegiate Athletic Association.

_____ . 1987–88. *Annual Reports.* Mission, KS: National Collegiate Athletic Association. (Cited as *NCAA Annual Reports.*)

───── . Various years. *Manual of the NCAA*. Mission, KS: National Collegiate Athletic Association. (Cited sometimes as *NCAA Manual*.)

───── . Various years and issues. *The NCAA News*. Mission, KS: National Collegiate Athletic Association.

───── . Various years. *Proceedings of the NCAA Annual Convention*. Mission, KS: National Collegiate Athletic Association. (Cited as *NCAA Proceedings*.)

National Collegiate Athletic Association v. Board of Regents of the University of Oklahoma et al. 1984. 83-271, Supreme Court of the United States.

National Collegiate Athletic Association, Petitioner, v. Jerry Tarkanian. 1989. 87-1061, Supreme Court of the United States.

Nelson, David. 1962. *Football Principles and Play*. New York: Ronald Press.

Newspaper Enterprise Association. Various years. *The World Almanac and Book of Facts*. New York: Newspaper Enterprise Association.

Noll, Roger G., ed. 1974. *Government and the Sports Business*. Washington, D.C.: Brookings Institution.

Olson, Mancur. 1965. *The Logic of Collective Action: Public Goods and the Theory of Groups*. Cambridge, MA: Harvard University Press.

Osborne, D. K. 1974. "Cartel Problems." *American Economic Review* 66 (December): 835–44.

Pacey, Patricia L. 1985. "The Courts and College Football: New Playing Rules off the Field?" *American Journal of Economics and Sociology* 44 (April): 145–55.

Porto, Brian. 1985. "Legal and Constitutional Challenges to the NCAA: The Limits of Adjudication in Intercollegiate Athletics." In Arthur Johnson and James Frey, eds., *Government and Sport: The Public Policy Issues*. Totowa, NJ: Rowman & Allanheld.

Raiborn, Mitchell H. 1986. *Revenues and Expenses of Intercollegiate Athletic Programs: Analysis of Financial Trends and Relationships, 1981–1985*. Mission, KS: National Collegiate Athletic Association.

Rasmussen, Eric. 1989. *Games and Information: An Introduction to Game Theory*. New York: Basil Blackwell.

Savage, Howard; Bentley, Harold W.; McGovern, John T.; and Smiley, Dean F. 1929. *American College Athletics*. Bulletin 23. New York: Carnegie Foundation for the Advancement of Teaching.

Scully, Gerald W. 1974. "Pay and Performance in Major League Baseball." *American Economic Review* 64:915–30.

————— . 1989. *The Business of Major League Baseball.* Chicago: University of Chicago Press.

Shughart, William F., II. 1990. *The Organization of Industry.* Homewood, IL: Richard Irwin.

Skousen, Clifford R., and Condie, Frank A. 1988. "Goalposts versus Test Tubes: Evaluating a Sports Program." *Management Accounting* 70 (November): 43–49.

Smith, Adam. 1937. *An Inquiry into the Nature and Causes of the Wealth of Nations.* Edwin Cannan, ed. New York: Modern Library.

Sperber, Murray. 1990. *College Sports, Inc.: The Athletic Department vs. the University.* New York: Holt.

*SPSS*ˣ *User's Guide.* 1986. 2d ed. New York: McGraw-Hill.

Stagg, Paul. 1946. "The Development of the National Collegiate Athletic Association in Relationship to Intercollegiate Athletics in the United States." Ph.D. dissertation, New York University.

Stigler, George J. 1964. "A Theory of Oligopoly." *Journal of Political Economy* 72 (February): 44–61.

————— . 1971. "The Theory of Economic Regulation." *Bell Journal of Economics and Management Science* 2 (Spring): 3–21.

————— . 1975. *The Citizen and the State: Essays on Regulation.* Chicago: University of Chicago Press.

Telander, Rick. 1989. *The Hundred Yard Line.* New York: Simon & Schuster.

Underwood, John. 1978. "The NCAA Goes on Defense." *Sports Illustrated,* October 9, pp. 20–29.

U.S. Department of Health, Education, and Welfare. 1973. *Digest of Education Statistics.* Washington, D.C.: U.S. Government Printing Office.

U.S. House of Representatives. 1978. "NCAA Enforcement Program." Hearings before the Subcommittee on Oversight and Investigations of the Committee on Interstate and Foreign Commerce, 96th Congress.

U.S. News and World Report, January 8, 1990.

U.S. Senate. 1977. "Amateur Sports Act Hearings." Hearing before the Committee on Commerce, Science, and Transportation. 96th Congress.

Washington Post. 1978–83. United Press International Poll. Washington Post Co., Washington, D.C.

Waterson, Michael. 1984. *Economic Theory of the Industry.* Cambridge: Cambridge University Press.

Wolff, Alexander, and Keteyian, Armen. 1990. *Raw Recruits.* New York: Pocket Books.

INDEX

Academic requirements for eligibility, 123–24, 128, 132
ACT, 61, 96
Air Force Academy, 165, 168
Alabama, University of, 76, 80, 85, 106, 120–21, 136, 142, 165, 168, 170, 172, 175
Alchian, Armen, 102, 177
Allen, W. R., 177
Alumni, revenues from, 78–79
Amateur Athletic Union, 147, 152
Amateur eligibility rules, 124
Amateur Sports Act, 147
American Bar Association, 45
American Broadcasting Company (ABC), 53, 58
American College Athletics, 44
American Council on Education, 177
American Medical Association, 45
American South Conference, 81
Arizona, University of, 108, 136, 165, 168, 170, 173–75
Arizona State University, 108, 165, 168, 170
Arkansas, University of, 85, 106, 119–20, 136, 142, 165, 168, 170, 173
Army, 165, 168, 170
Asch, Peter, 177
Athletes: compensation for, 4, 8, 9, 23–24, 26–27, 30, 32, 146, 149; eligibility requirements, 12, 95–96, 157; marginal value of, 92–93; organization of, 153–54; passivity of, 152; recruiting regulations,

93–94; recruitment of, 56–57; revenues generated by, 93
Athletic bylaws, 94
Athletics, demand for, 24
Atlantic Coast Conference, 51, 64, 78, 80–81, 125–26, 136
Auburn University, 46, 76, 78–79, 85, 93, 106, 165, 168, 170

Baker, W. J., 37, 124
Basketball, 55, 62; revenue from, 80–81
Baylor University, 165, 168, 170
Becher, Beverly, 177
Becker, Gary, 38
Beloit College, 172
Bentley, Harold, 180
Big East Conference, 64, 80–81
Big Eight Conference, 77, 80–81, 114, 120, 136
Big Sky Conference, 87
Big Ten Conference, 38, 43, 47–48, 64, 77–78, 80–81, 124, 136
Big West Conference, 81
Border Conference, 136
Boreland, Melvin B., xi, 73, 89, 177
Boston Celtics, 83
Boston College, 48, 93, 165, 168, 170
Boston Globe, 78
Bowl games, 55, 82
Bozik, Ed, 153
Bradley, Senator Bill, 155
Brigham Young University, 165, 168, 170, 174
Brown, Dale, 146

Browning, Edgar K., 7, 22, 177
Brown University, 172
Broyles, Frank, 55
Buchanan, James M., 177
Burger King, 9
Byers, Walter, 107, 147

Cairns, J., 7, 177
California, Berkeley, University of, 39, 165, 168, 170
California, Davis, University of, 175
California, Los Angeles, University of, 167–68, 170, 173–74
California, Santa Barbara, University of, 172–73
California State, Fresno, 174–75
Camp, Walter, 39
Canisius University, 158
Cantrell, Richard, xi
Carlton, Dennis, 177
Carnegie Foundation, 44, 46
Cartels: definition of, 6–7; study of, 6; theory of, 17–19, 21–22, 24–25, 27, 31, 33, 45
Chicago, University of, 45–46, 175
Chicago Bears, 13
Chu, Donald, 35, 177
Cincinnati, University of, 165, 170, 175
Citadel, the, 49, 172–73
Clark, Brent, 150
Clemson, University of, 13, 76, 122, 154, 165, 168, 170
Coaches: compensation of, 4, 8, 84, 91; rent seeking, 91
Colgate, 173
College athletics: as business, 4, 5; demand for, 14; expenses of, 83; as public good, 18–19
College Football Association, 15, 34, 68, 77–78
Colonial Conference, 81
Colorado, University of, 122, 165, 168, 170, 172–73
Colorado State University, 165, 170, 173–75

Columbia Broadcasting System (CBS), 29, 53, 64, 78
Columbia University, 37, 39
Condie, Frank A., 73, 89, 181
Cottingham, Clement, 78, 178
Coughlin, Cletus, 78, 177

Dallas Morning News, 151
Darth Vader, xi
Dartmouth College, 172–73
Davidson College, 158, 173
"Death penalty," 62
Demsetz, Harold, 102, 177
Denver, University of, 172
DePaul, 81
DePauw, 173
Dickey, Doug, 85
Dooley, Vince, 126
Drake University, 172
Duke University, 78, 157, 165, 168, 170
Dye, Pat, 85

Eagle Aloha Bowl, 82
East Carolina University, 165, 168
East Coast North Atlantic Conference, 81, 87
East Stroudsburg State, 175
Eckert, Ross D., 135, 178
Erekson, Homer O., 78, 177
Ewing, Patrick, 9, 92

Falla, Jack, 35, 37–39, 42, 50, 52–53, 55–56, 59, 67, 134, 139, 155, 178
Federal Trade Commission, 15
Feinstein, John, 145, 150–51, 178
Final Four, 80, 81, 93, 119
Fisk University, 175
Five-year rule, 57
Flath, Arnold W., 35, 39, 47, 178
Fleisher, A. F., 178
Florida, University of, 76, 78–79, 155, 165, 168, 170
Florida Citrus Bowl, 82
Florida State University, 64, 165, 169–70

Index

Flutie, Doug, 9, 93
Football, revenues from, 76
Football Rules Committee, 38
Ford, Dan, 154
Fort Valley College, 175
Franklin and Marshall University, 172
Freedom Bowl, 82
Freshman eligibility, 58

Georgetown University, 85, 93
Georgia, University of, 13, 28, 59, 69, 76, 78, 126, 136, 142, 165, 168, 170, 174
Georgia Tech, 165, 168, 170
Goff, Brian L., 37, 89, 124, 177–78
Graduation rates, 63
Green, Edward, 178
Greenspan, David, 53, 178
Grier, Kevin, xi

Hall of Champions, 91
Hall of Fame Bowl, 82
Hampton Institute, 173–74
Hart-Nibring, Nand, 78, 178
Harvard University, 37, 39, 172
Hayes, Woody, 92, 118
Hillard, Terry, 158
Hood, Robin, proposals, 57
Houston, University of, 116, 165, 168, 170, 172
Howard University, 174
Howsen, Roy, xi

Illinois, University of, 43, 118, 155, 165, 168, 170, 175
Independence Bowl, 82
Independent schools, 111
Indiana, University of, 85, 106, 165, 168, 170, 175
Infractions Committee, 72
Intercollegiate Athletic Association, 39
Intercollegiate Conference of Faculty Representatives, 38
Intercollegiate Football Association, 38

Iowa, University of, 43, 79, 165, 168, 170, 172–73
Iowa State University, 165, 168
Ivey, Mark, 178
Ivy League, 12, 87, 124, 126

Jackson, Bo, 9, 46, 93
Jenkins, Dan, 118, 124, 178
Jennet, N., 7, 177
John Hancock Sun Bowl, 82
Johns Hopkins University, 174

Kansas, University of, 49, 116, 136, 165, 168, 170
Kansas State University, 165, 170
Kent State University, 174–75
Kentucky, University of, 12, 85, 87, 106, 118–19, 151–52, 166, 170
Keteyian, Armen, 181
Knight, Bob, 85, 150
Knight Commission, 159–60; analysis of, 161
Knight Foundation, 159
Knox College, 173–74
Koch, James, 57, 178
Krzyzewski, Mike, 157

Lawrence, Paul R., 35, 38, 52, 55, 57, 136, 179
Lehigh University, 172
Lehman, Andrea, 179
Leonard, W. M., 57
Lewis, Guy M., 35, 39, 179
Lexington Herald-Leader, 151
Liberty Bowl, 82
Lincoln University, 174
Litigation: involving NCAA television contract, 55, 58; *National Collegiate Athletic Association v. Board of Regents of the University of Oklahoma et al.*, 59–60; *NCAA v. Tarkanian*, 63
Louisiana State University, 48, 76, 79, 166, 168, 170–71
Louisville University, 166, 168

MacCracken, Henry, 39
Maine, University of, 175
Maryland, University of, 48–49, 166, 168, 171
Massachusetts, University of, 172–73
Massachusetts Institute of Technology, 175
Mazda Gator Bowl, 82
McCallum, John D., 179
McCormick, Robert E., xi, 46, 101, 179
McGee, John, 22, 179
McGovern, John T., 180
McKenzie, Richard B., 7, 179
McMillan, Representative Tom, 155
Media, 146–51; role of, in reform, 149–51
Meiners, Roger, 179
Memphis State University, 146, 166, 168, 171
Metro Atlantic Conference, 81, 87
Miami, University of, 64, 166, 168
Michigan, University of, 4, 43, 48, 65, 76, 78, 80, 82, 84–85, 87, 89–91, 106, 121, 142, 166, 171–74; finances of, 55
Michigan State University, 43, 76, 118, 158, 166, 168, 171, 174–75
Mid-American Conference, 81
Mid-Continent Conference, 81
Mid-Eastern Conference, 81
Midwestern Conference, 81
Minnesota, University of, 122, 166, 169, 171
Mississippi, University of, 166, 168, 171
Mississippi State University, 79, 102, 138, 166, 169, 171
Missouri, University of, 49, 166, 168, 171, 173–74
Missouri Valley Conference, 81
Mobil Cotton Bowl, 82
Montana, University of, 173
Moss, John, 107
Mulenberg College, 175

National, 152
National Association of Basketball Coaches, 68, 157
National Association of Intercollegiate Athletics, 68
National Broadcasting Company (NBC), 52–53, 78
National Center for Education Statistics, 179
National Collegiate Athletic Association. See NCAA; NCAA convention; NCAA Council; NCAA enforcement; NCAA organization
National Collegiate Foundation, 80
National Invitational Tournament, 55–56
National Opinion Research Center, 52
Navy Academy, 166, 168, 171
NCAA, 179; Administrative Committee, 68; Annual Report, 102; and antitrust laws, 6, 10, 15; v. Board of Regents of the University of Oklahoma et al., 6, 10, 15, 53–54, 59–60, 156, 177, 180; and capital expenditures, 27–28; as cartel, 5–10; commercialization of, 44–45; Committee on Infractions, 24, 50, 60, 65, 70–72, 97, 102–3, 107, 134; committee structure, 42; compared to professional sports, 13–14; competition within, 12–13, 24–26; Compliance Committee, 48, 50; constitution, 41, 44; Council and Executive Committee, 49, 70–71; Council and Infractions Committee, 9, 11, 50, 57, 60, 65, 68, 70–72, 92, 97, 134–35, 138–43, 160; demand for, 30, 43–44, 54; expansion of, 43–45; formation of, 21; legal status of, 15; Letter of Intent, National, 56, 58; Manual of the NCAA, 56–57, 60–61, 63, 66, 68–71, 94–98; Membership Committee, 50; News, 72, 76, 80–81, 154; origins

of, 19; Presidents' Commission, 70–71, 146; "prisoners' dilemma," 18–19, 40; as provider of public goods, 18–20; realignment within, 64; Sanity Code, 47–51, 62; stability of, 13, 28; standardizing of, 37–38; startup costs, 21; v. Tarkanian, 15, 63, 134, 180; Television Committee, 8, 52, 55; Television Plan, 59, 78; Twelve-Point Plan, 49, 64; and U.S. Congress, 155; and violent play, 37–39

NCAA convention, 156–57

NCAA Council: control of, 134; football powers in, 142; membership in, 142, 172; role in reforms, 160

NCAA enforcement: action by school, 106; athletic recruitment, 56–57; athletic scholarships, 57; cheating, 137; conference rivalry, 136; contrasts in, 118–20; control of, 134–35; "death penalty," 62; development of, 43–50; and due process, 63, 98; economic model, 104; empirical test, 137–38; five-year rule, 57; and football powers, 120, 142–43; Infractions Committee, 50, 72; legal system, 154–55; LOGIT analysis of, 110–12; logrolling, 138; policy of, 12; probabilistic approach, 100; probation, 113; process monitoring, 32, 97, 100–103, 111, 133; racial bias, 62; reasons for, 51; recruitment, 137; redistribution, 104; regulation of, 97–98; repeat offenders, 116–17; sanctions, 11; Sanity Code, 46–48; secrecy of, 98, 107; Southwest Conference, 119; staff structure, 97, 102; and Tarkanian, Jerry, 154; television restrictions, 60, 65; theory of,31-32, 100–101; University of Oklahoma, 121; violation indicators, 101–2; winning percentages, 113–15

NCAA organization, 50, 70–71; affiliate members, 68; conferences, 68; corresponding members, 68; division structure, 68; Executive Committee, 71; faculty control within, 148; headquarters, 23; information gathering, 72; membership costs, 70; membership growth, 67; NCAA Council, 71; policy review, 145; Presidents' Commission, 70–71, 146; secrecy of, 98; stability of, 161; statement of purpose, 69; traditional powers, 133

Nebraska, University of, 76, 155, 158, 166, 168, 171

Nelson, David, 46, 180

Nevada, Las Vegas, University of, 15, 63, 85, 97, 155

New Mexico, University of, 136, 166, 169, 171

New Mexico State University, 128, 166, 168, 171

Newspaper Enterprise Association, 180

New York Stock Exchange, 84

New York Times, 39–40, 44–45, 48, 144, 149, 159

New York University, 39

Noll, Roger, 7, 180

North Carolina, University of, xi, 78, 85, 106, 120, 136, 142, 166, 171–73

North Carolina A&T, 158

North Carolina State University, 85, 106, 166, 168, 170, 174–75

North Central College and Secondary Schools Association, 11

Northeast Conference, 81

Northwestern University, 39, 43, 168, 170

Notre Dame, 13, 28, 34, 78, 81, 120–21, 150, 159, 161, 168, 170

Oberlin College, 172

Ohio State University, 43, 59, 76, 80, 118–21, 142, 168, 170, 174–75; violations by, 118

Ohio Valley Conference, 81, 118, 136
Ohio Wesleyan, 175
Oklahoma, University of, 6, 13, 15, 28, 59, 69, 76, 78, 106, 114, 120–22, 168, 170, 173, 175; probation of, 93, 114
Oklahoma A&M, 11, 49
Oklahoma State University, 11, 62, 168, 170
Olson, Mancur, 19, 180
Omaha World Leader, 78
Orange Bowl, 82
Oregon, University of, 168, 170, 174
Oregon State University, 168, 170, 173–74
Osborne, D. K., 22, 180
Osborne, Tom, 158

Pacey, Patricia L., 59, 180
Pacific, University of the, 175
Pacific Coast Conference, 47
Pacific 10 Conference, 77, 80, 108
Paterno, Joe, 85, 158
Peach Bowl, 52
Penn State, 64, 76, 85, 106, 121, 158, 168, 170, 173
Pennsylvania, University of, 52, 172–73
Perkins, Ray, 85
Perles, George, 158
Perloff, Jeffrey, 177
Phi Beta Kappa, 11
Philadelphia Inquirer, 150
Pittsburgh, University of, 153, 168, 170, 172, 174
Porter, Robert, 178
Posto, Brian, 59, 180
Princeton University, 37–39, 45
Principles of Conduct of Intercollegiate Athletics, 47
Proposition 42, 3, 29, 34, 42, 61, 123–24, 131–32, 145; votes for, 131
Proposition 48, 1, 3, 29, 34, 61, 96, 123–24, 131–32, 145, 152, 156; description of, 61; empirical anal-ysis, 126; reasons for, 124; rent seeking, 124–26
Pulitzer Prize, 149
Pulsinelli, Robert W., xi, 89
Purdue University, 43, 168, 170

Racism and academic eligibility, 123, 132
Raiburn, Mitchell H., 75, 180
Rasmussen, Eric, 28, 180
Reform: Amateur Athletic Union, 147; and compensation of athletes, 149; congressional pressure to, 146, 154–56; and the courts, 156; faculty control, 160; faculty efforts to, 148; failure of, 160–61; incen-tives against, 150–51; interest in, 144; Knight Commission, recom-mendations of, 144, 159; legislative pressure to, 155; and the media, 146, 149–51; NCAA convention (1991), 156; NCAA Council, 60; NCAA Presidents' Commission, 146, 150; policy review, 145; schol-arships, 156; television, 147; U.S. Olympic Committee, 147
Revenue, 72; accounting process, 73–74, 88–89; alumni contribu-tions, 78–79; athletic contribu-tions, 93; from basketball, 80–81, 93; from bowl games, 82; distri-bution of, 72; from football, 76; hiding of, 86–87, 89; reporting of, 73–74, 84, 86–87; sources, 78–88; surpluses, 89–91; from television, 77–78
Rice University, 136, 168, 170
Robert, Carol, xi
Robin Hood proposals, 57
Roosevelt, Theodore, 38–40
Rose Bowl, 82, 153
Rubinstein, Sharon, 178
Rutgers University, 37, 168, 170, 172

Sanity Code, 36, 120, 125–26, 132, 136, 145; description of, 46–48

San Jose State University, 172–73
Santa Clara, 172
Savage, Howard, 38, 180
Schembechler, Bo, 85
Scholarships, reforms involving, 156
Scholastic Aptitude Test (SAT), 46, 61, 96, 128, 132
Schultz, Dick, 9, 85, 158
Scully, Gerald W., 22, 86, 153, 180
Sea World Holiday Bowl, 82
Segrave, Jeffrey, 38, 177
Seneca, Joseph J., 177
Sherman Act, 15, 55, 59, 156
Sherrill, Jackie, 85
Shousen, Clifford R., 73, 89, 181
Shughart, W. F., xi, 22, 37, 124, 178, 181
Sloane, P. J., 7, 177
Smiley, Dean F., 180
Smith, Adam, 21, 187
Smith, Dean, 85
South Carolina, University of, xi, 64, 76, 168, 170
South Dakota State, 173, 175
Southeast Conference, 47, 64, 77–79, 81, 125–26, 136, 151
Southern California, University of, 78, 82, 168, 170, 172
Southern Conference, 81
Southern Methodist University, 62, 79, 116, 119, 136, 148, 152, 168, 170, 172
Southern Mississippi University, 167, 169
Southland Conference, 81
Southwest Conference, 47, 77–78, 81, 108, 119–20, 125–26, 136, 151, 155
Sports Illustrated, 85, 152
SPSS User's Guide, 181
Stagg, Amos Alonzo, 38
Stagg, Paul, 35, 38, 40–41, 181
Standard and Poor's, 84
Stanford University, 39, 166, 170, 172–73
Stigler, George J., 22, 102, 135, 181

Strozier, Robert, 45–46
Sullivan, Thomas E., 7, 179
Sun Belt Conference, 81
Sunkist Fiesta Bowl, 87
Supreme Court, 8, 10, 15, 55, 59–60, 63, 65, 77, 97, 134, 147–48, 156
Sutton, Eddie, 85
Swarthmore College, 173–74
Syracuse University, 166, 168, 170

Tarkanian, Jerry, 63, 85, 97, 154–55
Telander, Rich, 73, 181
Television contracts, 144, 147; and antitrust laws, 59, 70, 77, 156; competition for, 30, 52, 57, 69; history of, 52–53; litigation regarding, 55, 58–60, 77; restrictions on, 23, 52, 56, 60, 65; revenues from, 8, 10, 13, 15, 53–57, 60, 69, 77; Robin Hood proposals, 57
Television Committee, 52
Temple University, 164, 166, 170, 174–75
Tennessee, University of, 48, 76, 78, 85, 106, 136, 142, 158, 166, 168, 170, 173–74
Tennessee State University, 174–75
Texas, El Paso, University of, 128, 167, 169–70, 173
Texas, University of, 78, 119–20, 136, 142, 148, 155, 166, 168, 170, 175
Texas A&M University, 79, 85, 106, 122, 155, 166, 170, 172–74
Texas Christian University, 12, 103, 119–20, 122, 136, 167–68, 170, 172, 175
Texas Stadium, 148
Texas Tech University, 79, 136, 167–68, 170, 174–75
Thompson, John, 85
Thorpe, Jim, 124
Tinsley, Maurice, 46, 101, 179
Toledo, University of, 175
Tollison, Robert, 37, 124, 178–79

Trans America Conference, 81
Tucker, A. W., 18
Tufts University, 172, 174
Tulane University, 167–68, 170
Tullock, Gordon, 177
Tulsa, University of, 167, 169–70, 172
Turner Broadcasting, 53

Underwood, John, 181
Union College, 174
United Press International, 105
University Athletic Club of New York, 38
USA Today, 64, 85, 157–59
U.S. Congress, 63
U.S. Department of Health, Education, and Welfare, 181
USF&G Sugar Bowl, 82
U.S. House of Representatives, 105, 107, 110, 139, 155
U.S. News and World Report, 86, 181
U.S. Olympic Committee 146, 161
U.S. Senate, 147, 150, 181
Utah, University of, 167, 169, 171
Utah State University, 73, 89, 169, 171–72

Valparaiso College, 174
Valvano, Jim, 35
Vanderbilt University, 167, 169, 171–72
Villanova University, 49
Virginia, University of, 48–49, 85, 106, 125, 167, 169, 171
Virginia Military Institute, 49

Virginia Polytechnic Institute, 49, 167–68, 171–72

Wake Forest University, 167, 169, 171
Wards, Erwin, 102
Warner Cable Communication, 59
Washington, University of, 76, 106, 167–68, 171–72, 174–75
Washington Post, 73, 63, 105, 155, 181
Washington State University, 128, 167, 169, 171
Waterson, Michael, 22, 181
West Coast Conference, 81
Western Athletic Conference, 77–78, 81
Western Kentucky University, 73, 78, 89, 118–19
West Virginia University, 167–68, 171
Wichita State University, 148, 173
Wilbert, M. Leonard, 179
Williams College, 173–74
Wilson, Woodrow, 45
Wisconsin, University of, 43, 167–68, 171, 173
Wisely, Tom, xi
Witte, Al, 158
Wolff, Alexander, 181
Worcester Polytechnic Institute, 174–75
Wyoming, University of, 167–68, 171

Yale University, 37–39, 172
Yardley, Jonathan, 150